WEB APPLICATION DEVELOPMENT

ASP.NET WITH C#

HIMALI PATEL | KAUSHAL GOR

ISBN 979-888606210-6

Contents

Foreword

ASP.NET and C# are used every day by thousands of professional developers and engineers world-wide. It is more powerful which runs most successful websites and web applications in the world over WWW, and every day thousands of new professionals begin learning ASP.NET for the first time for web development. It is supported by an incredible developer community of books, blogs, user groups, forums, and developer websites that helps them to learn new things and to solve their problems. Our goal with Web Application Development using ASP.NET is to enable beginners and developers to easily build great ASP.NET web applications and websites that fully leverage the power of the technology, and which deliver a smoother and more interactive experience for end users. ASP.NET works with all modern browsers, and allows you to easily build great web applications and websites that work cross-platform on all operating systems. We are using Object Oriented Paradigm with C# in web development which makes our websites and web applications more powerful.

Preface

This book gives an overview of Web Development & Web programming from beginning to advance and with focus on ASP.NET (C#). ASP.NET is web development framework created by Microsoft. C# is an object oriented programming language by which we can do programming.The only way to learn programming is to do a lot of coding by yourself, and not only small code snippets with a few lines of code. You need to make large Web Applications and Websites. So in this we are Microsoft Visual Studio for web development and for database driven operations we are using Microsoft SQL Server. You are also going to learn advance concepts like LINQ, Stored Procedure, MVC and etc.It takes time and may be demanding, but that's the only way! The reward is knowledge that goes deep, and you will gain skills that is highly desired by the industry.

Acknowledgements

We hear and forget, we see and remember, we do and understand, goes on saying and how true it is. The practical knowledge always has the upper hand over the theoretical one and this is what we understood during this book. We are overwhelmed in all humbleness and gratefulness to acknowledge our depth to all those who have helped us to write a book, well above the level of simplicity and into something concrete.

We would like to express our special thanks of gratitude to Notion Press & Amazon for publishing this book.Any attempt at any level can 't be satisfactorily completed without the support and guidance of parents and friends.

We are greatly thankful to our beloved and wonderful friend Vibhuti Patel, who has constantly encouraged and motivated us while writing this book. She put us back on track whenever we deviated from our schedule of submitting the chapters. Without her support and encouragement, this book wouldn't have been possible.

Himali Patel
Kaushal Gor

Prologue

This book is aimed at anyone who wants to create dynamic websites or web applications with ASP.NET. Commonly, you'll have experience with a previous version of a programming language such as C, C++, VB or Java. If not, you should be familiar with basic programming concepts like variables, data types, looping, conditional structures, arrays and etc. Turing, or a completely different programming language. This is the only requirement for reading this book. Understanding markup languages like HTML and XHTML used to write web pages in ASP.NET, but it's not required. ASP.NET works at a higher level, allowing you to deal with full-featured web controls instead of raw web page markup.

CHAPTER I

Introduction

1.1 ASP.NET Introduction

- ASP.NET is the advanced version of ASP. It is a server side technology. ASP.NET is a web development platform, which provides a programming model, a comprehensive software infrastructure and various services required to build up robust web application for PC, as well as mobile devices.ASP.NET is run inside the IIS (Internet Information Services).
- ASP.NET works on top of the HTTP protocol and uses the HTTP commands and policies to set a browser-to-server two-way communication and cooperation.
- ASP.NET is a part of Microsoft .NET platform. ASP.NET applications are complied codes, written using the extensible and reusable components or objects present in .NET framework. These codes can use the entire hierarchy of classes in .NET framework.
- The ASP.NET application codes could be written in either of the following languages:
    - C#
    - Visual Basic .NET
    - Jscript
    - J#
- ASP.NET is used to produce interactive, data-driven web applications over the internet. It consists of a large number of controls like text boxes, buttons and labels for assembling,configuring and manipulating code to create HTML page.

• • •

1.2 ASP.NET Framework

- .NET is a framework that supports variety of languages & it provides the platform on which the languages can run.
- The .NET Framework is a comprehensive and an integrated programming model of the Windows operating system for building the next-gen applications. It is programmed with Dynamic Language Runtime (DLR), Common Language Runtime (CLR), Portable Class Library, Parallel Extension, Base Class Library (BCL) and WinRT.
- The .NET Framework also works alongside older Framework versions – .NET 3.5, 3.0, 2.0 – under the same hosting process.

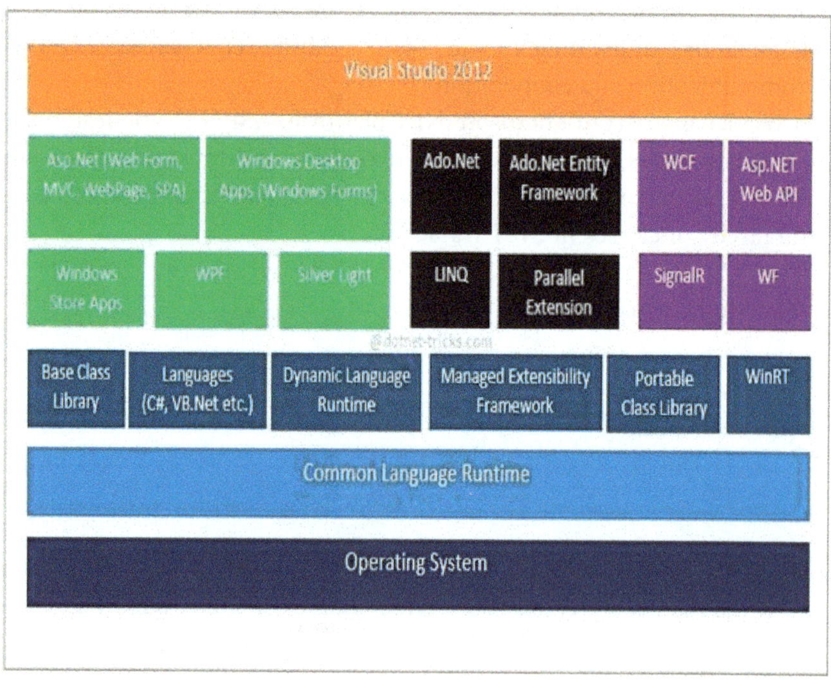

Figure 1 : .NET Framework 4.5 Architecture

Understanding the Components of Microsoft.NET Framework 4.5 Architecture:

- **Common Language Runtime (CLR)** : This provides the environment to execute the .NET Framework programs. Moreover, it also takes care of memory management and thread management of all the .NET programs.

- **Base Class Library (BCL)** : The BCL functions as a library of various functionalities which are common for all the languages using the .NET Framework, comprising of classes and interfaces of reusable types.

- **Portable Class Library (PCL)** : The PCL project in Visual Studio 2012 enables you to write and develop managed assemblies that function on multiple .NET Framework platforms. One can choose their platform such as .NET Framework, Silverlight, Windows Phone 7, or Xbox 360 platforms to target, using the Portable Class Library project.

- **Managed Extensibility Framework (MEF)** : The MEF is a library that enables the generation of lightweight and extensible applications. It allows the app developers to discover and employ extensions without the use of any configurations.

- **Dynamic Language Runtime (DLR)** : This gives the runtime environment for languages like python and so forth to perform under the full control of the CLR.

- **WinRT:** The WinRT or Windows Runtime APIs provide the user interface functions for developing Windows Store apps and allow access to various features of Windows 8 or Windows RT OS. It supports native C++, HTML, C#, VB.NET, as well as JavaScript and TypeScript.

- **ASP.NET** :This helps in creating rich internet-based, website applications.

- **Windows Store Apps (Metro Style Apps)** : This is a new app specially designed to run on Windows 8 devices and can take the advantage of the features of the new WinRT APIs. The .NET Framework supports the

Windows Store Apps which can only be distributed in the Windows 8 store.

- **Desktop Apps (Windows Forms) :** The Windows Desktop app is nothing but the traditional Windows application developed for the previous Windows versions like Windows XP, Windows Vista and Windows 7 but designated with a new name for Windows 8. The classic features of the Windows Desktop app include the Microsoft Office family products and notepad.

- **Windows Presentation Foundation (WPF) :** The WPF is used for rendering user interfaces to create applications with a rich userexperience. It comes with UI applications, 2D graphics, 3D graphics and multimedia. It is a resolution-independent engine that is built to take advantage of the hardware acceleration of modern graphics cards. Additionally, the WPF makes the UI perform faster.

- **Silverlight :** A web-based, cross-browser technology, Silverlight, enables designers and developers to create Rich Internet Applications (RIA) embedded in web pages.

- **ADO.NET :** It is a set of software components that allows the developers to create a Data Access Layer to access and manipulate data from underlying data sources like SQL Server, DB2, Oracle and so forth.

- **Language-Integrated Query or LINQ :** LINQ makes a query from various data sources such as SQL databases, XML documents, ADO.NET Datasets, Various Web services, Collections and Generics using Visual Basic or C#.

- **NET Entity Framework :** ADO.NET allows access into databases like SQL Server, Oracle, DB2 and so forth, and to accordingly process and update the data contained in them in an ORM fashion.

- **Parallel Extension :** With the use of Parallel Extension, developers can distribute their work code across various multiple processors in order to gain hardware advantage.

- **Windows Communication Foundation (WCF) :** WCF can be used to send across data as messages from a service endpoint to another using WS-* standards.

- **ASP.NET Web API :** ASP.NET Web API acts as a framework for creating HTTP services that are of use to a wide range of clients such as mobiles, iPhone and tablets and browsers.

- **SignalR :** ASP.NET SignalR is a library that facilitates the process of adding real-time web functionality to applications by making it less complicated. Real-time web functionality allows the server code push content to connected clients instantaneously, rather than having to wait for a client to request for new data.

- **Visual Studio 2012 :** The Visual Studio IDE is a library of tools that facilitate the developers in writing and modifying the code for various programs, alongside detecting and rectifying errors. It is also used for developing Windows Store apps, mobile apps, desktop apps, ASP.NET web apps, and web services.

• • •

1.3 The Origin of .NET Technology

- Microsoft started development on the .NET Framework in the late 1990s originally under the name of Next Generation Windows Services (NGWS).
- By late 2001 the first beta versions of .NET 1.0 were released. The first version of .NET Framework was released on 13 February 2002, bringing managed code to Windows NT 4.0, 98, 2000, ME and XP.
- Since the first version, Microsoft has released nine more upgrades for .NET Framework, seven of which have been released along with a new version of Visual Studio.
- Two of thesc upgrades, .NET Framework 2.0 and 4.0, have upgraded Common Language Runtime (CLR). New versions of .NET Framework

replace older versions when the CLR version is the same.

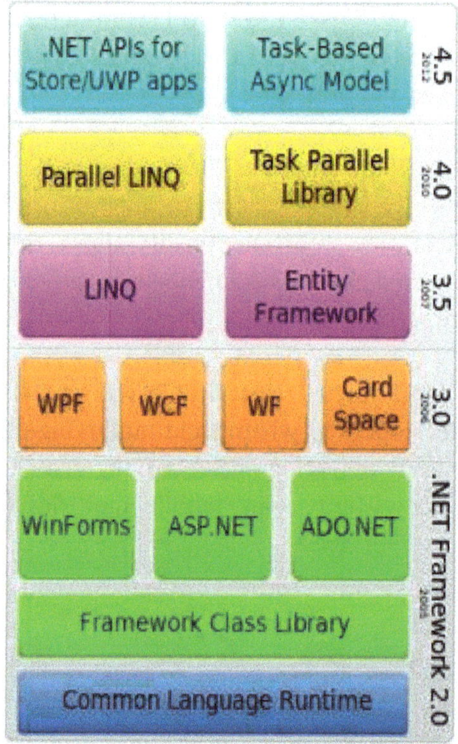

Figure 2 : The Origin of .NET Technology

• • •

1.4 Common Language Runtime (CLR)

The .NET Framework provides a run-time environment called the common language runtime, which runs the code and provides services that make the development process easier.

- Managed Code: Code that you develop with a language compiler that targets the runtime is called managed code. In short, all IL are managed code.
- The Common Language Runtime (CLR) is an Execution Environment. It works as a layer between Operating Systems and the applications written in .NET languages that conforms to the Common Language Specification (CLS).
- The main function of Common Language Runtime (CLR) is to convert the Managed Code (IL) into native code and then execute the Program. The Managed Code compiled only when it needed, that is it converts the appropriate instructions when each function is called The Common Language Runtime (CLR) 's Just In Time (JIT) compilation converts Intermediate Language (MSIL) to native code on demand at application run time.
- When an assembly starts running, the JIT (Just In Time) compiler in the Common Language Runtime converts the IL in the assembly to efficient machine code. It is this code that is actually executed.

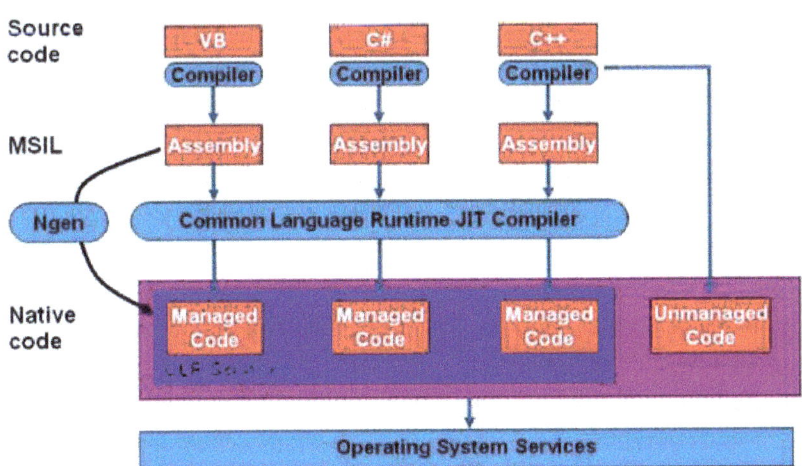

Figure 3 : Common Language Runtime Execution Model

Following are the functionality of the CLR:

- Garbage collection
- Code access security
- Code verification
- IL(managed code) to native translators and optimizers

• • •

1.5 Common Type System (CTS)

It describes set of data types that can be used in different .NET languages in common. (i.e), CTS ensures that objects written in different .NET languages can interact with each other.

- For Communicating between programs written in any .NET complaint language, the types have to be compatible on the basic level.
- The common type system supports two general categories of types:

1. **Value types**

    ◦ Value types directly contain their data, and instances of value types are either allocated on the stack or allocated inline in a structure.
    ◦ Value types can be built-in (implemented by the runtime), user-defined, or enumerations.

2. **Reference types:**

    ◦ Reference types store a reference to the value's memory address, and are allocated on the heap.
    ◦ Reference types can be self-describing types, pointer types, or interface types. The type of a reference type can be determined from values of self-describing types.
    ◦ Self-describing types are further split into arrays and class types. The class types are user-defined classes, boxed value types, etc.

• • •

1.6 Common Language Specification (CLS)

A Common Language Specification (CLS) is a document that says how computer programs can be turned into MSIL code. When several languages use the same bytecode, different parts of a program can be written in different languages.

- Microsoft uses a Common Language Specification for their .NET Framework. To fully interact with other objects regardless of the language they were used in, objects must expose to callers only those features that are common to all the languages they must exchange information with.
- Microsoft has defined CLS which are nothing but guidelines for languages to follow so that it can communicate with other .NET languages in a unified manner.
- Common Language Specification (CLS) defines a subset of Common Type System (CTS). Common Type System (CTS) describes a set of types that can use different .NET languages have in common, which ensure that objects written in different languages can interact with each other.
- Most of the members defined by types in the .NET Framework Class Library (FCL) are Common Language Specification (CLS) compliant Types .

• • •

1.7 Microsoft Intermediate Language(MSIL)

MSIL stands for Microsoft Intermediate Language. It is also known as Intermediate Language (IL) or Common Intermediate Language (CIL).

- During the compile time , the compiler convert the source code into Microsoft Intermediate Language (MSIL). Microsoft Intermediate

Language (MSIL) is a CPU-independent set of instructions that can be efficiently converted to the native code. During the runtime the Common Language Runtime (CLR)'s Just In Time (JIT) compiler converts the Microsoft Intermediate Language (MSIL) code into native code to the Operating System.

- When a compiler produces Microsoft Intermediate Language (MSIL), it also produces Metadata. The Microsoft Intermediate Language (MSIL) and Metadata are contained in a portable executable (PE) file .
- Microsoft Intermediate Language (MSIL) includes instructions for loading, storing, initializing, and calling methods on objects, as well as instructions for arithmetic and logical operations, control flow, direct memory access, exception handling, and other operations.
- The main Advantage of using MSIL is it provides equal performance for multiple language programming, as code is compiled to native code.

• • •

1.8 Just-In-Time Compiler (JIT)

Just-in-time compiler is a compiler used to convert the Common Intermediate Language (CIL) code into native code (also called machine code) that is processed by machine.

- While compiling of .NET program, its code is converted into Common Intermediate Language code that is done by Common Language Runtime. But while executing the program this CIL code is converted into Machine code or Native code that is done by JIT Compiler.
- The Common Language Runtime (CLR) provides various Just In Time compilers (JIT) and each works on a different architecture depending on Operating System. That is why the same Microsoft Intermediate Language (MSIL) can be executed on different Operating Systems without rewrite the source code.
- Just In Time (JIT) compilation preserves memory and save time during application initialization. Just In Time (JIT) compilation is used to run at high speed, after an initial (starting) phase of slow interpretation. Just In Time Compiler (JIT) code generally provides better performance than

interpreters.

• • •

1.9 Framework Base Classes

The .NET Framework class library is a library of classes, interfaces, and value types that provide access to system functionality. It is the foundation on which .NET Framework applications, components, and controls are built.

- The class library holds a huge amount of prewritten code that all the applications you create with Visual Basic, Visual C++, C#, and other Visual Studio languages build on.
- This library is organized into namespaces that contain functionally related groups of classes. These namespaces are divided among different categories, such as data access, common types, debugging, file access, network communication, security, Windows applications, Web applications, Web services, XML data etc.
- Following are some important namespaces that are defined in the .NET Framework class library:

Namespaces	**Description**
System	This namespace includes all common datatypes, string values, arrays, methods for data conversion, and methods related to mathematical operations.
System.Data, System.Data.Common, System.Data.OleDb, System.Data.SqlClient, System.Data.SqlTypes	These namespaces are used to access a database, perform commands on a database, and retrieve and manipulate a database.
System.Diagnostics	This namespace is used to debug and trace the execution of an application.
System.Windows.Forms, System.Windows.Forms.Design	These namespaces are used to create Windowsbased applications using Windows user interface components.

Table 1 : .NET Framework class library

• • •

1.10 Page Lifecycle

When the user changes a control that has auto postback set to true:

1. Java script is invoked and the page is resubmitted
2. ASP.NET recreates page object from .aspx file
3. ASP.NET retrieves state information from hidden fields and updates controls
4. Execute Page_load event handler
5. Execute appropriate event handlers
6. Execute page_unload event handler and render page
7. Send page to client

Page Processing Steps

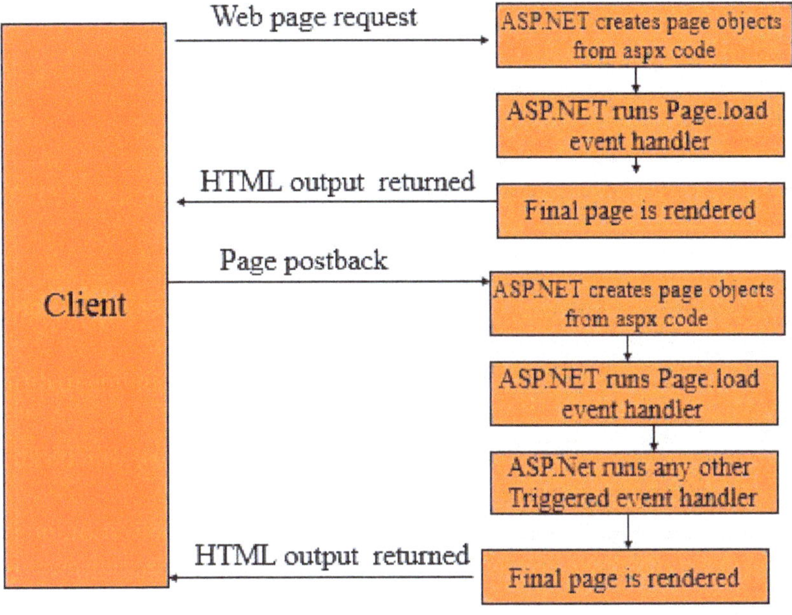

Figure 4 : Page Life Cycle

CHAPTER II

ASP.NET Controls, UI Design & Coding

2.1 ASP.NET Server Controls

ASP.NET server Controls are the primary Controls used in ASP.NET. These Controls can be grouped into the following categories:

- **Validation Controls** : These are used to validate user input and they work by running client-side script.
- **Data source Controls** : These Controls provides data binding to different data sources.
- **Data view Controls** : These are various lists and tables, which can bind to data from data sources for displaying.
- **Personalization Controls** : These are used for personalization of a page according to the user preferences, based on user information.
- **Login and security Controls** : These Controls provide user authentication.
- **Navigation Controls** : These Controls help in navigation. For example, menus, tree view etc.
- **Rich Controls** : These Controls implement special features. For example, AdRotator, File Upload, and Calendar Control.

The syntax for using server Controls is:

<asp:ControlType ID ="ControlID" runat="server" Property1=value1 [Property2=value2] />

Properties of the Server Controls

- ASP.NET server Controls with a visual aspect are derived from the WebControl class and inherit all the properties, events, and methods of this class.

- The WebControl class itself and some other server Controls that are not visually rendered are derived from the System.Web.UI.Control class. For example, PlaceHolder Control or XML Control.
- ASP.NET server Controls inherit all properties, events, and methods of the WebControl and System.Web.UI.Control class.

The following table shows common to all server Controls:

CONTROL	DESCRIPTION
Label	**Represents a label control**
ListBox	**Represents a list box control**
CheckBox	**Represents a Check box control**
Calendar	Represents a calendar control
ImageButton	Represents an image button control
TableCell	Represents a table cell
Panel	Represents a panel control
DataList	Represents a data list control
TextBox	**Represents a text box control**
Image	**Represents an image control**
CheckBoxList	Represents a list box with check boxes
Button	**Represents a button control**
HyperLink	Represents a hyperlink control
TableRow	Represents a row of a table
RadioButtonList	Represents a list box with radio button controls
DataGrid	Represents a data grid control
DropDownList	**Represents a drop-down list control**
AdRotator	Represents an ad rotator control
RadioButton	**Represents a radio button control**
LinkButton	Represents a link button control
Table	Represents a table control
Repeater	Represents a repeater control

Table 2-2 : Server Control

Properties of the Server Controls

- ASP.NET server Controls with a visual aspect are derived from the WebControl class and inherit all the properties, events, and methods of this class.
- The WebControl class itself and some other server Controls that are not visually rendered are derived from the System.Web.UI.Control class. For example, PlaceHolder Control or XML Control.
- ASP.NET server Controls inherit all properties, events, and methods of the WebControl and System.Web.UI.Control class.

The following table shows the inherited properties, common to all server Controls:

Property	Description
AccessKey	Pressing this key with the Alt key moves focus to the control.
Attributes	It is the collection of arbitrary attributes (for rendering only) that do not correspond to properties on the control.
BackColor	Background color.
BindingContainer	The control that contains this control's data binding.
BorderColor	Border color.
BorderStyle	Border style.
BorderWidth	Border width.
CausesValidation	Indicates if it causes validation.
ChildControlCreated	It indicates whether the server control's child controls have been created.
ClientID	Control ID for HTML markup.
Context	The HttpContext object associated with the server control.
Controls	Collection of all controls contained within the control.
ControlStyle	The style of the Web server control.
CssClass	CSS class
DataItemContainer	Gets a reference to the naming container if the naming container implements IDataItemContainer.

DataKeysContainer	Gets a reference to the naming container if the naming container implements IDataKeysControl.
DesignMode	It indicates whether the control is being used on a design surface.
DisabledCssClass	Gets or sets the CSS class to apply to the rendered HTML element when the control is disabled.
Enabled	Indicates whether the control is grayed out.
EnableTheming	Indicates whether theming applies to the control.
EnableViewState	Indicates whether the view state of the control is maintained.
Events	Gets a list of event handler delegates for the control.
Font	Font.
Forecolor	Foreground color.
HasAttributes	Indicates whether the control has attributes set.
HasChildViewState	Indicates whether the current server control's child controls have any saved view-state settings.
Height	Height in pixels or %.
ID	Identifier for the control.
IsChildControlStateCleared	Indicates whether controls contained within this control have control state.
IsEnabled	Gets a value indicating whether the control is enabled.

IsTrackingViewState	It indicates whether the server control is saving changes to its view state.
IsViewStateEnabled	It indicates whether view state is enabled for this control.
LoadViewStateById	It indicates whether the control participates in loading its view state by ID instead of index.
Page	Page containing the control.
Parent	Parent control.
RenderingCompatibility	It specifies the ASP.NET version that the rendered HTML will be compatible with.
Site	The container that hosts the current control when rendered on a design surface.
SkinID	Gets or sets the skin to apply to the control.
Style	Gets a collection of text attributes that will be rendered as a style attribute on the outer tag of the Web server control.
TabIndex	Gets or sets the tab index of the Web server control.
TagKey	Gets the HtmlTextWriterTag value that corresponds to this Web server control.
TagName	Gets the name of the control tag.
TemplateControl	The template that contains this control.
TemplateSourceDirectory	Gets the virtual directory of the page or control containing this control.
ToolTip	Gets or sets the text displayed when the mouse pointer hovers over the web server control.
UniqueID	Unique identifier.
ViewState	Gets a dictionary of state information that saves and restores the view state of a server control across multiple requests for the same page.
ViewStateIgnoreCase	It indicates whether the StateBag object is case-insensitive.
ViewStateMode	Gets or sets the view-state mode of this control.
Visible	It indicates whether a server control is visible.
Width	Gets or sets the width of the Web server control.

Table 2-3 : Server Controls Properties

Methods of the Server Controls

The following table provides the methods of the server Controls:

Method	Description
AddAttributesToRender	Adds HTML attributes and styles that need to be rendered to the specified HtmlTextWriterTag.
AddedControl	Called after a child control is added to the Controls collection of the control object.
AddParsedSubObject	Notifies the server control that an element, either XML or HTML, was parsed, and adds the element to the server control's control collection.
ApplyStyleSheetSkin	Applies the style properties defined in the page style sheet to the control.
ClearCachedClientID	Infrastructure. Sets the cached ClientID value to null.
ClearChildControlState	Deletes the control-state information for the server control's child controls.
ClearChildState	Deletes the view-state and control-state information for all the server control's child controls.
ClearChildViewState	Deletes the view-state information for all the server control's child controls.
CreateChildControls	Used in creating child controls.
CreateControlCollection	Creates a new ControlCollection object to hold the child controls.
CreateControlStyle	Creates the style object that is used to implement all style related properties.
DataBind	Binds a data source to the server control and all its child controls.
DataBind(Boolean)	Binds a data source to the server control and all its child controls with an option to raise the DataBinding event.
DataBindChildren	Binds a data source to the server control's child controls.
Dispose	Enables a server control to perform final clean up before it is released from memory.

Dispose	Enables a server control to perform final clean up before it is released from memory.
EnsureChildControls	Determines whether the server control contains child controls. If it does not, it creates child controls.
EnsureID	Creates an identifier for controls that do not have an identifier.
Equals(Object)	Determines whether the specified object is equal to the current object.
Finalize	Allows an object to attempt to free resources and perform other cleanup operations before the object is reclaimed by garbage collection.
FindControl(String)	Searches the current naming container for a server control with the specified id parameter.
FindControl(String, Int32)	Searches the current naming container for a server control with the specified id and an integer.
Focus	Sets input focus to a control.
GetDesignModeState	Gets design-time data for a control.
GetType	Gets the type of the current instance.
GetUniqueIDRelativeTo	Returns the prefixed portion of the UniqueID property of the specified control.
HasControls	Determines if the server control contains any child controls.
HasEvents	Indicates whether events are registered for the control or any child controls.
IsLiteralContent	Determines if the server control holds only literal content.
LoadControlState	Restores control-state information.
LoadViewState	Restores view-state information.
MapPathSecure	Retrieves the physical path that a virtual path, either absolute or relative, maps to.
MemberwiseClone	Creates a shallow copy of the current object.

MergeStyle	Copies any nonblank elements of the specified style to the web control, but does not overwrite any existing style elements of the control.
OnBubbleEvent	Determines whether the event for the server control is passed up the page's UI server control hierarchy.
OnDataBinding	Raises the data binding event.
OnInit	Raises the Init event.
OnLoad	Raises the Load event.
OnPreRender	Raises the PreRender event.
OnUnload	Raises the Unload event.
OpenFile	Gets a Stream used to read a file.
RemovedControl	Called after a child control is removed from the controls collection of the control object.
Render	Renders the control to the specified HTML writer.
RenderBeginTag	Renders the HTML opening tag of the control to the specified writer.
RenderChildren	Outputs the contents of a server control's children to a provided HtmlTextWriter object, which writes the contents to be rendered on the client.
RenderContents	Renders the contents of the control to the specified writer.
RenderControl(HtmlTextWriter)	Outputs server control content to a provided HtmlTextWriter object and stores tracing information about the control if tracing is enabled.
RenderEndTag	Renders the HTML closing tag of the control into the specified writer.
ResolveAdapter	Gets the control adapter responsible for rendering the specified control.
SaveControlState	Saves any server control state changes that have occurred since the time the page was posted back to the server.
SaveViewState	Saves any state that was modified after the TrackViewState method was invoked.
SetDesignModeState	Sets design-time data for a control.
ToString	Returns a string that represents the current object.
TrackViewState	Causes the control to track changes to its view state so that they can be stored in the object's view state property.

Table 2-4 : Server Controls Methods

• • •

2.2 ASP.NET HTML Server Controls

The HTML server Controls are basically the standard HTML Controls enhanced to enable server side processing. The HTML Controls such as the header tags, anchor tags, and input elements are not processed by the server but are sent to the browser for display.

They are specifically converted to a server Control by adding the attribute runat="server" and adding an id attribute to make them available for server-side processing

For example, consider the HTML input Control:

<input type="text" size="40">

It could be converted to a server Control, by adding the runat and id attribute:

<input type="text" id="testtext" size="40" runat="server">

Advantages of using HTML Server Controls

- Although ASP.NET server Controls can perform every job accomplished by the HTML server Controls, the later Controls are useful in the following cases:
- Using static tables for layout purposes.
- Converting a HTML page to run under ASP.NET

The following table describes the HTML server Controls:

Control Name	HTML tag
HtmlHead	<head>element
HtmlInputButton	<input type=button|submit|reset>
HtmlInputCheckbox	<input type=checkbox>
HtmlInputFile	<input type = file>
HtmlInputHidden	<input type = hidden>
HtmlInputImage	<input type = image>
HtmlInputPassword	<input type = password>
HtmlInputRadioButton	<input type = radio>
HtmlInputReset	<input type = reset>
HtmlText	<input type = text|password>
HtmlImage	<img> element
HtmlLink	<link> element
HtmlAnchor	<a> element
HtmlButton	<button> element
HtmlButton	<button> element
HtmlForm	<form> element
HtmlTable	<table> element
HtmlTableCell	<td> and <th>
HtmlTableRow	<tr> element
HtmlTitle	<title> element
HtmlSelect	<select< element
HtmlGenericControl	All HTML controls not listed

Table 2-5 : HTML server Controls

• • •

2.3 ASP.NET - Basic Controls

Button Controls

ASP.NET provides three types of button Control:

- Button : It displays text within a rectangular area.
- Link Button : It displays text that looks like a hyperlink.
- Image Button : It displays an image.

When a user clicks a button, two events are raised: Click and Command.

Basic syntax of button Control:

<asp:Button ID="Button1" runat="server" onclick="Button1_Click" Text="Click" / >

Common properties of the Button Control:

Property	Description
Text	The text displayed on the button. This is for button and link button controls only.
ImageUrl	For image button control only. The image to be displayed for the button.
AlternateText	For image button control only. The text to be displayed if the browser cannot display the image.
CausesValidation	Determines whether page validation occurs when a user clicks the button. The default is true.
CommandName	A string value that is passed to the command event when a user clicks the button.
CommandArgument	A string value that is passed to the command event when a user clicks the button.
PostBackUrl	The URL of the page that is requested when the user clicks the button.

Table 2-6 : Button Control Properties

Text Boxes and Labels

Text box Controls are typically used to accept input from the user. A text box Control can accept one or more lines of text depending upon the settings of the TextMode attribute.

Label Controls provide an easy way to display text which can be changed from one execution of a page to the next. If you want to display text that does not change, you use the literal text.

Basic syntax of text Control:

<asp:TextBox ID="txtstate" runat="server" ></asp:TextBox>

Common Properties of the Text Box and Labels:

Property	Description
TextMode	Specifies the type of text box. SingleLine creates a standard text box, MultiLIne creates a text box that accepts more than one line of text and the Password causes the characters that are entered to be masked. The default is SingleLine.
Text	The text content of the text box.
MaxLength	The maximum number of characters that can be entered into the text box.
Wrap	It determines whether or not text wraps automatically for multi-line text box; default is true.
ReadOnly	Determines whether the user can change the text in the box; default is false, i.e., the user can not change the text.
Columns	The width of the text box in characters. The actual width is determined based on the font that is used for the text entry.
Rows	The height of a multi-line text box in lines. The default value is 0, means a single line text box.

Table 2.7 : Text Box and Labels Properties

The mostly used attribute for a label Control is 'Text', which implies the text displayed on the label.

Check Boxes and Radio Buttons

A check box displays a single option that the user can either check or uncheck and radio buttons present a group of options from which the user can select just one option.

To create a group of radio buttons, you specify the same name for the GroupName attribute of each radio button in the group. If more than one group is required in a single form, then specify a different group name for each group.

If you want check box or radio button to be selected when the form is initially displayed, set its Checked attribute to true. If the Checked attribute is set to true for multiple radio buttons in a group, then only the last one is considered as true.

Basic syntax of check box:

<asp:CheckBox ID= "chkoption" runat= "Server"> </asp:CheckBox>

Basic syntax of radio button:

<asp:RadioButton ID= "rdboption" runat= "Server"> </asp: RadioButton>

Common properties of check boxes and radio buttons:

Property	Description
Text	The text displayed next to the check box or radio button.
Checked	Specifies whether it is selected or not, default is false.
GroupName	Name of the group the control belongs to.

Table 2-8 : Check Boxes and Radio Buttons Properties

List Controls

ASP.NET provides the following Controls :

- Drop-down list,
- List box,
- Radio button list,
- Check box list,

- Bulleted list.

These Control let a user choose from one or more items from the list. List boxes and drop-down lists contain one or more list items. These lists can be loaded either by code or by the ListItemCollection editor.

Basic syntax of list box Control:

```
<asp:ListBox ID="ListBox1" runat="server" AutoPostBack="True"
OnSelectedIndexChanged="ListBox1_SelectedIndexChanged">
</asp:ListBox>
```

Basic syntax of drop-down list Control:

```
<asp:DropDownList ID="DropDownList1" runat="server"
AutoPostBack="True"
OnSelectedIndexChanged="DropDownList1_SelectedIndexChanged">
</asp:DropDownList>
```

Common properties of list box and drop-down Lists:

Property	Description
Items	The collection of ListItem objects that represents the items in the control. This property returns an object of type ListItemCollection.
Rows	Specifies the number of items displayed in the box. If actual list contains more rows than displayed then a scroll bar is added.
SelectedIndex	The index of the currently selected item. If more than one item is selected, then the index of the first selected item. If no item is selected, the value of this property is -1.
SelectedValue	The value of the currently selected item. If more than one item is selected, then the value of the first selected item. If no item is selected, the value of this property is an empty string ("").
SelectionMode	Indicates whether a list box allows single selections or multiple selections.

Table 2-9 : List box and Drop-down Lists Properties

Common properties of each list item objects:

Property	Description
Text	The text displayed for the item.
Selected	Indicates whether the item is selected.
Value	A string value associated with the item.

Table 2-10 : Common Properties of each list item

The ListItemCollection

The ListItemCollection object is a collection of ListItem objects. Each ListItem object represents one item in the list. Items in a ListItemCollection are numbered from 0.

When the items into a list box are loaded using strings like: lstcolor.Items.Add("Blue"), then both the Text and Value properties of the list item are set to the string value you specify. To set it differently you must create a list item object and then add that item to the collection.

The ListItemCollection Editor is used to add item to a drop-down list or list box. This is used to create a static list of items. To display the collection editor, select edit item from the smart tag menu, or select the Control and then click the ellipsis button from the Item property in the properties window.

Common Properties of ListItemCollection :

Property	Description
Item(integer)	A ListItem object that represents the item at the specified index.
Count	The number of items in the collection.

Table 2-11 : ListItemCollection Properties

Common methods of ListItemCollection :

Methods	Description
Add(string)	Adds a new item at the end of the collection and assigns the string parameter to the Text property of the item.
Add(ListItem)	Adds a new item at the end of the collection.
Insert(integer, string)	Inserts an item at the specified index location in the collection, and assigns string parameter to the text property of the item.
Insert(integer, ListItem)	Inserts the item at the specified index location in the collection.
Remove(string)	Removes the item with the text value same as the string.
Remove(ListItem)	Removes the specified item.
RemoveAt(integer)	Removes the item at the specified index as the integer.
Clear	Removes all the items of the collection.
FindByValue(string)	Returns the item whose value is same as the string.
FindByValue(Text)	Returns the item whose text is same as the string.

Table 2-12 : ListItemCollection Methods

Radio Button list and Check Box list

A radio button list presents a list of mutually exclusive options. A check box list presents a list of independent options. These Controls contain a collection of ListItem objects that could be referred to through the Items property of the Control.

Basic syntax of radio button list:

```
<asp:RadioButtonList ID="RadioButtonList1" runat="server"
AutoPostBack="True"
OnSelectedIndexChanged="RadioButtonList1_SelectedIndexChanged">
</asp:RadioButtonList>
```

Basic syntax of check box list:

```
<asp:CheckBoxList ID="CheckBoxList1" runat="server"
AutoPostBack="True"
OnSelectedIndexChanged="CheckBoxList1_SelectedIndexChanged">
</asp:CheckBoxList>
```

Common properties of check box and radio button lists:

Property	Description
RepeatLayout	This attribute specifies whether the table tags or the normal html flow to use while formatting the list when it is rendered. The default is Table.
RepeatDirection	It specifies the direction in which the controls to be repeated. The values available are Horizontal and Vertical. Default is Vertical.
RepeatColumns	It specifies the number of columns to use when repeating the controls; default is 0.

Table 2-13 : Common Properties of check box and radio button lists

Bulleted lists and Numbered lists

The bulleted list Control creates bulleted lists or numbered lists. These Controls contain a collection of ListItem objects that could be referred to through the Items property of the Control.

Basic syntax of a bulleted list:

<asp:BulletedList ID="BulletedList1" runat="server"> </asp:BulletedList>

Common properties of the bulleted list:

Property	Description
BulletStyle	This property specifies the style and looks of the bullets, or numbers.
RepeatDirection	It specifies the direction in which the controls to be repeated. The values available are Horizontal and Vertical. Default is Vertical.
RepeatColumns	It specifies the number of columns to use when repeating the controls; default is 0.

Table 2-14 : Common Properties of the bulleted list

HyperLink Control

The HyperLink Control is like the HTML <a> element.

Basic syntax for a hyperlink Control:

<asp:HyperLink ID="HyperLink1" runat="server"> HyperLink </asp:HyperLink>

It has the following important properties:

Property	Description
ImageUrl	Path of the image to be displayed by the control.
NavigateUrl	Target link URL.
Text	The text to be displayed as the link.
Target	The window or frame which loads the linked page.

Table 2-15 : Hyperlink Conrol Properties

Image Control

The image Control is used for displaying images on the web page, or some alternative text, if the image is not available.

Basic syntax for an image Control:

<asp:Image ID="Image1" runat="server">

It has the following important Properties:

Property	Description
AlternateText	Alternate text to be displayed in absence of the image.
ImageAlign	Alignment options for the control.
ImageUrl	Path of the image to be displayed by the control.

Table 2-16 : Image Control Properties

• • •

2.4 Web.config file

- The web.config file uses a predefined XML format. The entire content of the file is nested in a root <configuration> element. Inside this element are several more subsections, some of which you'll never change, and others which are more important.
- Here's the basic skeletal structure of the web.config file, with the three most important sections highlighted in bold:

```
<?xml version="1.0" ?>
<configuration>
<configSections>...</configSections>
<appSettings>...</appSettings>
<connectionStrings>...</connectionStrings>
<system.web>...</system.web>
<system.codedom>...</system.codedom>
<system.webServer>...</system.webServer>
</configuration>
```

- Note that the web.config file is case-sensitive, like all XML documents, and starts every setting with a lowercase letter. This means you cannot write <AppSettings> instead of <appSettings>.
- As a web developer, there are three sections in the web.config file that you'll work with.
- The <appSettings> section allows you to add your own miscellaneous pieces of information.
- The <connectionStrings> section allows you to define the connection information for accessing a database. And
- The <system.web> section holds every ASP.NET setting you'll need to configure.
- Inside the <system.web> element are separate elements for each aspect of website configuration.
- **Storing Custom Settings in the web.config File:**
- ASP.NET also allows you to store your own settings in the web.config file, in an element called <appSettings>.
- Here's the basic structure:

```
<?xml version="1.0" ?>
<configuration>
...
<appSettings>
<!-- Custom application settings go here. -->
</appSettings>
...
<system.web>
<!-- ASP.NET Configuration sections go here. -->
</system.web>
...
</configuration>
```

- The custom settings that you add are written as simple string variables. You might want to use a special web.config setting for several reasons:
- To centralize an important setting that needs to be used in many different pages: For example, you could create a variable that stores a database query. Any page that needs to use this query can then retrieve this value and use it.
- To make it easy to quickly switch between different modes of operation: For example, you might create a special debugging variable. Your web pages could check for this variable and, if it's set to a specified value, output additional information to help you test the application.
- To set some initial values: Depending on the operation, the user might be able to modify these values, but the web.config file could supply the defaults.
- You can enter custom settings using an <add> element that identifies a unique variable name (key) and the variable contents (value).

2.5 Global.asax in ASP.NET

- The Global.asax file, also known as the ASP.NET application file, is an optional file that contains code for responding to application-level events raised by ASP.NET or by HttpModules.
- The Global.asax file resides in the root directory of an ASP.NET-based application. The Global.asax file is parsed and dynamically compiled by

ASP.NET.

- The Global.asax file itself is configured so that any direct URL request for it is automatically rejected; external users cannot download or view the code written within it.
- The Global.asax file does not need recompilation if no changes have been made to it. There can be only one Global.asax file per application and it should be located in the application's root directory only.
- The Global.asax contains two types of events those are

1. **Events which are fired for every request**
2. **Events which are not fired for every request**

1) Events which are fired for every request :

- **Application_BeginRequest():** This is called at the start of every request.
- **Application_AuthenticateRequest():** This is called before authentication is performed.
- **Application_AuthorizeRequest():** This is called when the authentication stage is completed.
- **Application_ResolveRequestCache():** This is often used in conjunction with output caching. Then the request is sent to its assigned handler.
- **Application_AcquirrRequestState():** This is called just before session-specific data is retrieved for the client and is used to populate session collection.
- **Application_PreRequestHandlerExecute():** This is called before the appropriate HTTP handler executes the rcquest.
- The handler now executes the request. The code of your ASP.NET web form large is now executed and the HTML is now rendered.
- **Application_PostRequestHandlerExecute():** This is called just after the request is handled by its appropriate HTTP handler
- **Application_ReleaseRequestState():** This is called when the session-specific information is about to be serialized from the session collection so that its available for the next request.
- **Application_UpdateRequestCache():** This is called just before the information is added to the output cache
- **Application_EndRequest():** This is called at the end of the request right before the objects are released and reclaimed. It's the place to add your cleanup code.

2) Events which are not fired for every request

- **Application_Start():** This is called when the application first starts up and the application domain is created. This is place for you to insert application wide initialization code.
- **Session_Start():** This method is invoked each time a new session begins. This is often used to initialize user specific information. Some developers also use this to count the number of current active user session in the application.
- **Application_Error():** This is invoked whenever an unhandled exception occurs in the application. You may want to use this to perform some custom error handling logic application wide.
- **Session_End():** This is called when user session ends. A session ends when your code releases it explicitly or its idle time exceeds the set expiry timeout. Developers add the code here to clean up any related data.
- **Application_End():** This method is invoked just before an application ends. the end of an application can occur because IIS is shut down or the application is transitioning to anew domain in response to file updates or process recycling.
- **Application_Disposed():** This method is called sometime after the application is shut down and the garbage collector is about to reclaim the memory it occupies. Note that it is already too late to perform critical cleanup at this point of time but you may want to add code here to verify that resources have been released as last which is safe proof.

How to careet a Global.asax file

Global.asax file don't create normally; you need to add it by yourself.

How to ?

Open Visual Studio
Create a new website
Go to the Solution Explorer
Add New Item
Global Application Class
Add

Your Global.asax file look like this

```
<%@ Application Language="C#" %>
<script runat="server">
    void Application_Start(object sender, EventArgs e)
    {
        // Code that runs on application startup
    }
    void Application_End(object sender, EventArgs e)
    {
        //  Code that runs on application shutdown
    }
    void Application_Error(object sender, EventArgs e)
    {
        // Code that runs when an unhandled error occurs
    }
    void Session_Start(object sender, EventArgs e)
    {
        // Code that runs when a new session is started
    }
    void Session_End(object sender, EventArgs e)
    {
        // Code that runs when a session ends.
        // Note: The Session_End event is raised only when the sessionstate
        // is set to InProc in the Web.config file. If session mode is set t
        // or SQLServer, the event is not raised.
    }
</script>
```

After that you need to add a class in your project.

Right clicking App_Code
Add New Item
Class
name it Global.cs
Add

nherit the newly generated by System.Web.HttpApplication and copy all the method created Global.asax to Global.cs and also add an inherit attribute to the Global.asax file

Now your Global.asax will look like following:

```
public class Global : System.Web.HttpApplication
{
    public Global()
    {
        //
        // TODO: Add constructor logic here
        //
    }

    void Application_Start(object sender, EventArgs e)
    {
        // Code that runs on application startup

    }
    /// Many other events like begin request...e.t.c, e.t.c
}
```

• • •

2.6 Programming ASP.NET Web Pages

Webpage:

Understanding Dynamic Compilation:

- Strangely enough, when you create an ASP.NET page, you are actually creating the source code for a .NET class. You are creating a new instance of the System.Web.UI.Page class. The entire contents of an ASP.NET page, including all script and HTML content, are compiled into a .NET class.
- When you request an ASP.NET page, ASP.NET Framework checks for a .NET class that corresponds to the page. If a corresponding class does not exist, the Framework automatically compiles the page into a new class and stores the compiled class (the assembly) in the Temporary ASP.NET Files folder located at the following path:
- \WINDOWS\Microsoft.NET\Framework\v4.0.30128\Temporary ASP.NET Files
- The next time anyone requests the same page in the future, the page is not compiled again. The previously compiled class is executed, and the results are returned to the browser.
- The compiled class is preserved in the Temporary ASP.NET Files folder until the source code for your application is modified.
- When the class is added to the Temporary ASP.NET Files folder, a file dependency is created between the class and the original ASP.NET page. If the ASP.NET page is modified in any way, the corresponding .NET class is automatically deleted. The next time someone requests the page, the Framework automatically compiles the modified page source into a new .NET class.
- This process is called dynamic compilation, which enables ASP.NET applications to support thousands of simultaneous users. Unlike an ASP Classic page, for example, an ASP.NET page does not need to be parsed and compiled every time it is requested. An ASP.NET page is compiled only when an application is modified.

Understanding Control Trees:

- You can think of an ASP.NET page as a bag of Controls. More accurately, because some Controls might contain child Controls, you can think of an

ASP.NET page as a Control tree.

Using Code-Behind Pages:

- The ASP.NET Framework (and Visual Web Developer) enables you to create two different types of ASP.NET pages. You can create both single-file and two-file ASP.NET pages.
- In a single-file ASP.NET page, a single file contains both the page code and page Controls. The page code is contained in a <script runat="server"> tag.
- As an alternative to a single-file ASP.NET page, you can create a two-file ASP.NET page. A two-file ASP.NET page is normally referred to as a code-behind page. In a code-behind page, the page code is contained in a separate file.
- Handling Page Events:
- Whenever you request an ASP.NET page, a particular set of events is raised in a particular sequence. This sequence of events is called the page execution lifecycle.
- For example, we have already used the Page Load event in previous code samples. You normally use the Page Load event to initialize the properties of Controls contained in a page. However, the Page Load event is only one event supported by the Page class.

Following is the sequence of events raised whenever you request a page:

- PreInit
- Init
- InitComplete
- PreLoad
- Load
- LoadComplete
- PreRender
- PreRenderComplete
- SaveStateComplete
- Unload

- Different things happen and different information is available at different stages in the page execution lifecycle. **For example,**
- View State is not loaded until after the InitComplete event. Data posted to the server from a form Control, such as a TextBox Control, is also not available until after this event.
- Ninety-nine percent of the time, you won't handle any of these events except for the Load and the PreRender events. The difference between these two events is that the Load event happens before any Control events, and the PreRender event happens after any Control events.

Using the Page.IsPostBack Property:

- The Page class includes a property called the IsPostBack property, which you can use to detect whether the page has already been posted back to the server.
- Because of View State, when you initialize a Control property, you do not want to initialize the property every time a page loads. Because View State saves the state of Control properties across page posts, you typically initialize a Control property only once, when the page first loads.
- Many Controls don't work correctly if you reinitialize the properties of the Control with each page load. In these cases, you must use the IsPostBack property to detect whether the page has been posted.

Debugging and Tracing ASP.NET Pages

- The sad fact of life is that you spend the majority of your development time when building applications debugging the application. In this section, you learn how to get detailed error messages when developing ASP.NET pages. You also learn how you can display custom trace messages that you can use when debugging a page.

Debugging ASP.NET Pages

- If you need to view detailed error messages when you execute a page, you need to enable debugging for either the page or your entire application. You can enable debugging for a page by adding a Debug="true" attribute to the <%@ Page %> directive.

• • •

2.7 Introduction of an ASP.NET Application

- It's sometimes difficult to define exactly what a web application is. Unlike a traditional desktop program (which users start by running a stand-alone EXE file), ASP.NET applications are almost always divided into multiple web pages. This division means a user can enter an ASP.NET application at several different points or follow a link from the application to another part of the website or another web server. So, does it make sense to consider a website as an application?
- In ASP.NET, the answer is yes. Every ASP.NET application shares a common set of resources and configuration settings. Web pages from other ASP.NET applications don't share these resources, even if they're on the same web server. Technically speaking, every ASP.NET application is executed inside a separate *application domain*. Application domains are isolated areas in memory, and they ensure that even if one web application causes a fatal error, it's unlikely to affect any other application that is currently running on the same computer. Similarly, application domains restrict a web page in one application from accessing the in-memory information of another application. Each web application is maintained separately and has its own set of cached, application, and session data.
- The standard definition of an ASP.NET application describes it as a combination of files, pages, handlers, modules, and executable code that can be invoked from a virtual directory (and, optionally, its subdirectories) on a web server. In other words, the virtual directory is the basic grouping structure that delimits an application.

ASP.NET File Types:

ASP.NET applications can include many types of files.

File Name	Description
Ends with .aspx	These are ASP.NET web pages (the .NET equivalent of the .asp file in an ASP application). They contain the user interface and, optionally, the underlying application code. Users request or navigate directly to one of these pages to start your web application.
Ends with .asmx	These are ASP.NET web services—collections of methods that can be called over the Internet. Web services work differently than web
	pages, but they still share the same application resources, configuration settings, and memory.
web.config	This is the XML-based configuration file for your ASP.NET application. It includes settings for customizing security, state management, memory management, and much more.
Global.asax	This is the global application file. You can use this file to define global variables (variables that can be accessed from any web page in the web application) and react to global events (such as when a web application first starts).
Ends with .cs:	These are code-behind files that contain C# code. They allow you to separate the application logic from the user interface of a web page.

Table 2-17 : ASP.NET Files Types

ASP.NET Application Directories:

- Every web application should have a well-planned directory structure. For example, you'll probably want to store images in a separate folder from where you store your web pages. Or you might want to put public ASP.NET pages in one folder and restricted ones in another so you can apply different security settings based on the directory.
- Along with the directories you create, ASP.NET also uses a few specialized subdirectories, which it recognizes by name. Keep in mind that you won't see all these directories in a typical application. Visual Studio will prompt you to create them as needed.

Directory	Description
Bin	Contains all the compiled .NET components (DLLs) that the ASP.NET web application uses. For example, if you develop a custom component for accessing a database, you'll place the component here. ASP.NET will automatically detect the assembly, and any page in the web application will be able to use it.
App_Code	Contains source code files that are dynamically compiled for use in your application. You can use this directory in a similar way as the Bin
	directory; the only difference is that you place source code files here instead of compiled assemblies.
App_GlobalResources	Stores global resources that are accessible to every page in the web application. This directory is used in localization scenarios, when you need to have a website in more than one language. Localization isn't covered in this book, although you can refer to *Pro ASP.NET 3.5 in VB* (Apress, 2007) for more information.
App_LocalResources	Serves the same purpose as App_GlobalResources, except these resources are accessible to a specific page only.
App_WebReferences	Stores references to web services that the web application uses.
App_Data	Stores data, including SQL Server 2005 Express Edition database files and XML files. Of course, you're free to store data files in other directories.
App_Themes	Stores the themes that are used by your web application.

Table 2-18 : ASP.NET Application Directories

2.8 The Page Class

- Every web page is a custom class that inherits from System.Web.UI.Page. By inheriting from this class, your web page class acquires a number of properties and methods that your code can use.

Property	Description
IsPostBack	This Boolean property indicates whether this is the first time the page is being run (False) or whether the page is being resubmitted in response to a control event, typically with stored view state information(True). You'll usually check this property in the Page.Load event handler to ensure that your initial web page initialization is only performed once.
EnableViewState	When set to False, this overrides the EnableViewState property of the contained controls, thereby ensuring that no controls will maintain state information.
Application	This collection holds information that's shared between all users in your website. For example, you can use the Application collection to count the number of times a page has been visited.
Session	This collection holds information for a single user, so it can be used in different pages. For example, you can use the Session collection to store the items in the current user's shopping basket on an e-commerce website.
Cache	This collection allows you to store objects that are time-consuming to create so they can be reused in other pages or for other clients. This technique, when implemented properly, can improve performance of your web pages.
Request	This refers to an HttpRequest object that contains information about the current web request.
Response	This refers to an HttpResponse object that represents the response ASP.NET will send to the user's browser.
Server	This refers to an HttpServerUtility object that allows you to perform a few miscellaneous tasks. For example, it allows you to encode text so that it's safe to place it in a URL or in the HTML markup of your page.
User	User If the user has been authenticated, this property will be initialized with user information.

Table 2-19 : The Page Class Properties

• • •

2.9 Data types

Datatypes :

- Data Types in a programming language describes that what type of data a variable can hold . CSharp is a strongly typed language, therefore every variable and object must have a declared type.
- The CSharp type system contains three Type categories. They are

A)**Value Types**

B) Reference Types
C) Pointer Types .

- In CSharp it is possible to convert a value of one type into a value of another type . The operation of Converting a Value Type to a Reference Type is called Boxing and the reverse operation is called Unboxing.

A) Value Type

- Value type variables can be assigned a value directly. They are derived from the class System.ValueType.
- The value types directly contain data. Some examples are int, char, and float, which stores numbers, alphabets, and floating point numbers, respectively. When you declare an int type, the system allocates memory to store the value.
- The following table lists the available value types in C#:

Type	Represents	Range	Default Value
bool	Boolean value	True or False	False
byte	8-bit unsigned integer	0 to 255	0
char	16-bit Unicode character	U +0000 to U +ffff	'\0'
decimal	128-bit precise decimal values with 28-29 significant digits	$(-7.9 \times 10^{28}$ to $7.9 \times 10^{28}) / 10^{0 \text{ to } 28}$	0.0M
double	64-bit double-precision floating point type	$(+/-)5.0 \times 10^{-324}$ to $(+/-)1.7 \times 10^{308}$	0.0D
float	32-bit single-precision floating point type	-3.4×10^{38} to $+ 3.4 \times 10^{38}$	0.0F
Int	32-bit signed integer type	-2,147,483,648 to 2,147,483,647	0
Long	64-bit signed integer type	-9,223,372,036,854,775,808 to 9,223,372,036,854,775,807	0L
sbyte	8-bit signed integer type	-128 to 127	0
short	16-bit signed integer type	-32,768 to 32,767	0
Uint	32-bit unsigned integer type	0 to 4,294,967,295	0
Ulong	64-bit unsigned integer type	0 to 18,446,744,073,709,551,615	0
Ushort	16-bit unsigned integer type	0 to 65,535	0

Table 2-20 : Value Types

B) Reference Type

- The reference types do not contain the actual data stored in a variable, but they contain a reference to the variables.
- In other words, they refer to a memory location. Using multiple variables, the reference types can refer to a memory location. If the data in the memory location is changed by one of the variables, the other variable automatically reflects this change in value.
- **Example of built-in reference types are: object, dynamic, and string.**

1. Object Type

- The Object Type is the ultimate base class for all data types in C# Common Type System (CTS). Object is an alias for System.Object class.

The object types can be assigned values of any other types, value types, reference types, predefined or user-defined types. However, before assigning values, it needs type conversion.

- When a value type is converted to object type, it is called boxing and on the other hand, when an object type is converted to a value type, it is called unboxing.
- object obj;
- obj = 100; // this is boxing

2. Dynamic Type

- You can store any type of value in the dynamic data type variable. Type checking for these types of variables takes place at run-time.
- Syntax for declaring a dynamic type is:
- dynamic <variable_name> = value;
- For example,
- dynamic d = 20;
- Dynamic types are similar to object types except that type checking for object type variables takes place at compile time, whereas that for the dynamic type variables takes place at run time.

3. String Type

- The String Type allows you to assign any string values to a variable. The string type is an alias for the System.String class. It is derived from object type. The value for a string type can be assigned using string literals in two forms: quoted and @quoted.
- For example,
- String str = "Tutorials Point";
- A @quoted string literal looks as follows:
- @"Tutorials Point";
- The user-defined reference types are: class, interface, or delegate. We will discuss these types in later chapter.

C) Pointer Type

- Pointer type variables store the memory address of another type. Pointers in C# have the same capabilities as the pointers in C or C++.

- Syntax for declaring a pointer type is:

  type* identifier; For example, char* cptr; int* iptr;

• • •

2.10 Variables

- A variable is nothing but a name given to a storage area that our programs can manipulate. Each variable in C# has a specific type, which determines the size and layout of the variable's memory the range of values that can be stored within that memory and the set of operations that can be applied to the variable.
- The basic value types provided in C# can be categorized as:

Type	Example
Integral types	sbyte, byte, short, ushort, int, uint, long, ulong, and char
Floating point types	float and double
Decimal types	Decimal
Boolean types	true or false values, as assigned
Nullable types	Nullable data types

Table 2-21 : Variable Value Tupes

C# also allows defining other value types of variable such as **enum** and reference types of variables such as **class**, which we will cover in subsequent chapters.

Defining Variables

Syntax for variable definition in C# is:

<data_type> <variable_list>;

Here, data_type must be a valid C# data type including char, int, float, double, or any userdefined data type, and variable_list may consist of one or more identifier names separated by commas.

Some valid variable definitions are shown here:

int i, j, k;

char c, ch; float f, salary; double d;

You can initialize a variable at the time of definition as:

int i = 100;

Initializing Variables

Variables are initialized (assigned a value) with an equal sign followed by a constant expression. The general form of initialization is:

variable_name = value;

Variables can be initialized in their declaration. The initializer consists of an equal sign followed by a constant expression as:

<data_type> <variable_name> = value;

Some examples are:

int d = 3, f = 5; /* initializing d and f. */ byte z = 22; /* initializes z. */

double pi = 3.14159; /* declares an approximation of pi. */ char x = 'x'; /* the variable x has the value 'x'. */

• • •

2.11 Statements

- There are two type of statements in ASP.NET as below:

  1. Decision making/Conditional statements
  2. Loop statements

1. Decision making/Conditional statements

- Decision making structures requires the programmer to specify one or more conditions to be evaluated or tested by the program, along with a statement or statements to be executed if the condition is determined to be true, and optionally, other statements to be executed if the condition is determined to be false.

types of decision making statements:

Statement	Description
if statement	An **if statement** consists of a boolean expression followed by one or more statements.
if...else statement	An **if statement** can be followed by an optional **else statement**, which executes when the boolean expression is false.
nested if statements	You can use one **if** or **else if** statement inside another **if** or **else if** statement(s).
switch statement	A **switch** statement allows a variable to be tested for equality against a list of values.

Table 2-22 : Statements

1. If statement:

- An **if** statement consists of a boolean expression followed by one or more statements.

  Syntax

```
if(boolean_expression)
{
  /* statement(s) will execute if the boolean expression is true */
}
```

- If the boolean expression evaluates to **true**, then the block of code inside the if statement is executed. If boolean expression evaluates to **false**, then the first set of code after the end of the if statement(after the closing curly brace) is executed.

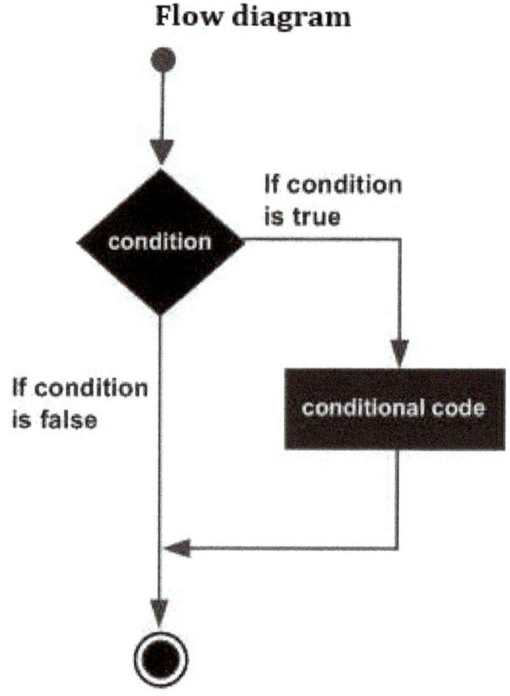

Figure 2-1 : Flow Daigram of If Statement

Example:

```
int num1, num2;
num1 = 100;
num2 = 200;
            if (num1 > num2)
            {
                    Label1.Text = "Num1 is greater than num2";
            }
```

2. If...else statement :

- **if** statement can be followed by an optional **else** statement, which executes when the boolean expression is false.

Syntax :

```
if(boolean_expression)
{
  /* statement(s) will execute if the boolean expression is true */
} else
{
  /* statement(s) will execute if the boolean expression is false */
}
```

If the boolean expression evaluates to **true**, then the **if block** of code is executed, otherwise **else block** of code is executed.

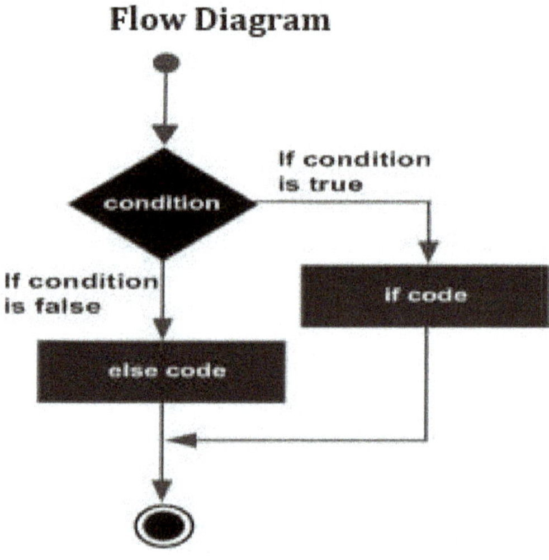

Figure 2-2 : Flow Daigram of if_else Statement

Example:

```
int num1, num2;
    num1 = 100;
    num2 = 200;

            if (num1 > num2)
            {
                    Label1.Text = "Num1 is greater than num2";
            }
            else
            {
                    Label1.Text = "Num2 is greater than num1";
            }
```

3. *if...else if...else Statement*

- An if statement can be followed by an optional else if...else statement, which is very useful to test various conditions using single if...else if statement.
- When using if, else if, else statements there are few points to keep in mind.
- An if can have zero or one else's and it must come after any else if's.
- An if can have zero to many else if's and they must come before the else.
- Once an else if succeeds, none of the remaining else if's or else's will be tested.

Syntax

```
if(boolean_expression 1)
{
  /* Executes when the boolean expression 1 is true */
}
else if( boolean_expression 2)
{
  /* Executes when the boolean expression 2 is true */
}

else if( boolean_expression 3)
{
  /* Executes when the boolean expression 3 is true */
} else
{
  /* executes when the none of the above condition is true */
}
```

Example:

```
if (totalMarks >= 80) {
        MessageBox.Show("Got Higher First Class ");
    }
    else if (totalMarks >= 60) {
        MessageBox.Show("Got First Class ");
    }
    else if (totalMarks >= 40){
        MessageBox.Show("Just pass only");
    }
    else {
        MessageBox.Show("Failed");
}
```

4. Nested if :

- It is always legal in C# to **nest** if-else statements, which means you can use one if or else if statement inside another if or else if statement(s).

  Syntax

```
if( boolean_expression 1)
{
  /* Executes when the boolean expression 1 is true */
if(boolean_expression 2)
  {
    /* Executes when the boolean expression 2 is true */
  }
}
```

- You can nest **else if...else** in the similar way as you have nested *if* statement.

Example:

-

```
int a = 100;
int b = 200;

    /* check the boolean condition */
if (a == 100)
    {
      /* if condition is true then check the following */
if (b == 200)
      {
        /* if condition is true then print the following */
        Message box.Show("Value of a is 100 and b is 200");
      }
```

5. *Switch case:*

- A **switch** statement allows a variable to be tested for equality against a list of values. Each value is called a case, and the variable being switched on is checked for each **switch case**.

Syntax

```
switch(expression) {    case
constant-expression  :
   statement(s);   break; /*
optional */   case constant-
expression  :
   statement(s);
break; /* optional */

  /* you can have any number of case statements */
default : /* Optional */   statement(s);
}
```

The following rules apply to a **switch** statement:

- The **expression** used in a **switch** statement must have an integral or enumerated type, or be of a class type in which the class has a single conversion function to an integral or enumerated type.
- You can have any number of case statements within a switch. Each case is followed by the value to be compared to and a colon.
- The **constant-expression** for a case must be the same data type as the variable in the switch, and it must be a constant or a literal.

- When the variable being switched on is equal to a case, the statements following that case will execute until a **break** statement is reached.
- When a **break** statement is reached, the switch terminates, and the flow of Control jumps to the next line following the switch statement.
- Not every case needs to contain a **break**. If no **break** appears, the flow of Control will *fall through* to subsequent cases until a break is reached.
- A **switch** statement can have an optional **default** case, which must appear at the end of the switch. The default case can be used for performing a task when none of the cases is true. No **break** is needed in the default case.

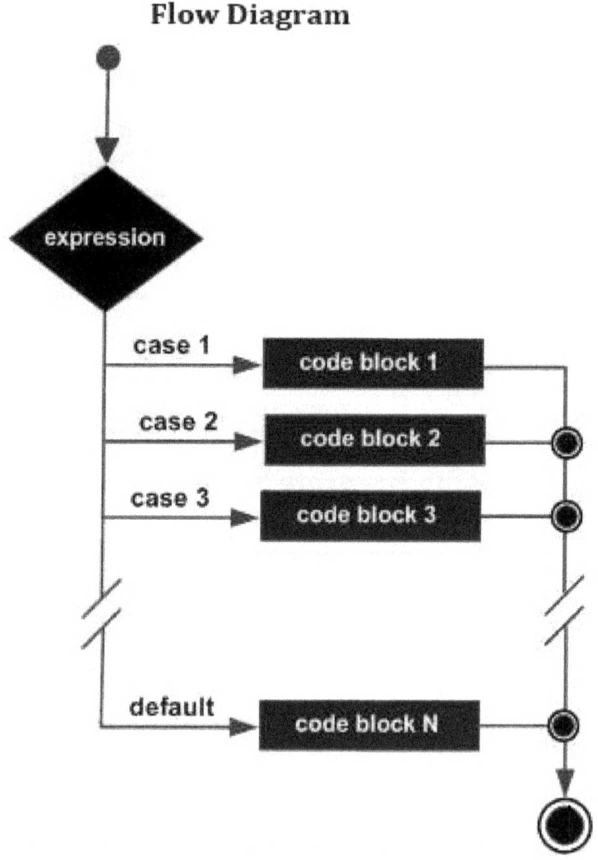

Figure 2-3 : Flow Daigram of Switch

Example:

```
string val;
 switch (val)
          {
             case "A+":
                MessageBox.Show("Excellent !!");
    break;           case "A":
                MessageBox.Show("Very Good  !!");
    break;           case "B":
                MessageBox.Show("Good  !!");
    break;           case "C":
                MessageBox.Show("Passed !!");
    break;           case "D":
                MessageBox.Show("Failed !!");
    break;           default:
                MessageBox.Show("Out of range !!");
    break;
        }
```

2. Loop Statement

- A loop statement allows us to execute a statement or a group of statements multiple times.

Types of loop statements:

Loop Type	Description
while loop	It repeats a statement or a group of statements while a given condition is true. It tests the condition before executing the loop body.
for loop	It executes a sequence of statements multiple times and abbreviates the code that manages the loop variable.
do...while loop	It is similar to a while statement, except that it tests the condition at the end of the loop body

Table 2-4 : Lopp Statement Types

1) While Loop :

- **while** loop statement in C# repeatedly executes a target statement as long as a given condition is true.

Syntax

```
while(condition)
{
  statement(s);
}
```

- Here, **statement(s)** may be a single statement or a block of statements. The **condition** may be any expression, and true is any non-zero value. The loop iterates while the condition is true.
- When the condition becomes false, program Control passes to the line immediately following the loop.

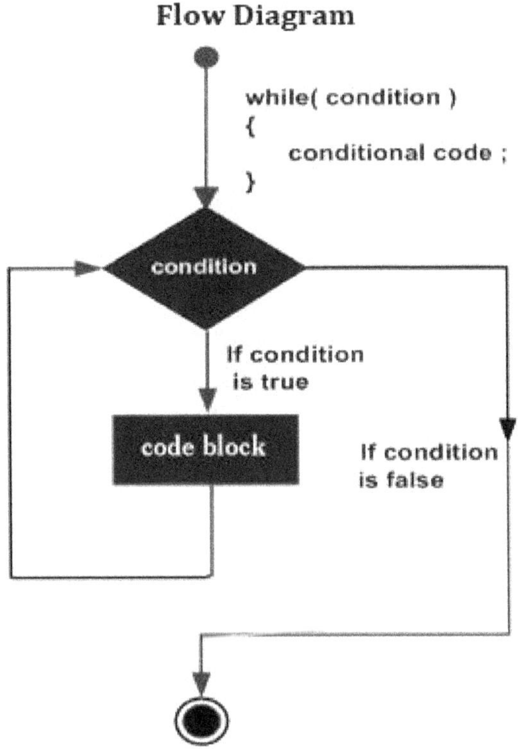

Figure 2-4 : Flow Daigram of While Statement

Here, key point of the *while* loop is that the loop might not ever run. When the condition is tested and the result is false, the loop body is skipped and the first statement after the while loop is executed.

```
int count = 1;
                    while (count < = 4)
                    {
              MessageBox.Show("The value of i is : " + count);
    count = count + 1;
                    }
```

2) For Loop

- A **for** loop is a repetition Control structure that allows you to efficiently write a loop that needs to execute a specific number of times.

Syntax

```
for ( init; condition; increment )
{
  statement(s);
}
```

Here is the flow of Control in a for loop:

- The **init** step is executed first, and only once. This step allows you to declare and initialize any loop Control variables. You are not required to put a statement here, as long as a semicolon appears.
- Next, the **condition** is evaluated. If it is true, the body of the loop is executed. If it is false, the body of the loop does not execute and flow of Control jumps to the next statement just after the for loop.
- After the body of the for loop executes, the flow of Control jumps back up to the **increment** statement. This statement allows you to update any loop Control variables. This statement can be left blank, as long as a

semicolon appears after the condition.

- The condition is now evaluated again. If it is true, the loop executes and the process repeats itself (body of loop, then increment step, and then again testing for a condition).

After the condition becomes false, the for loop terminates.

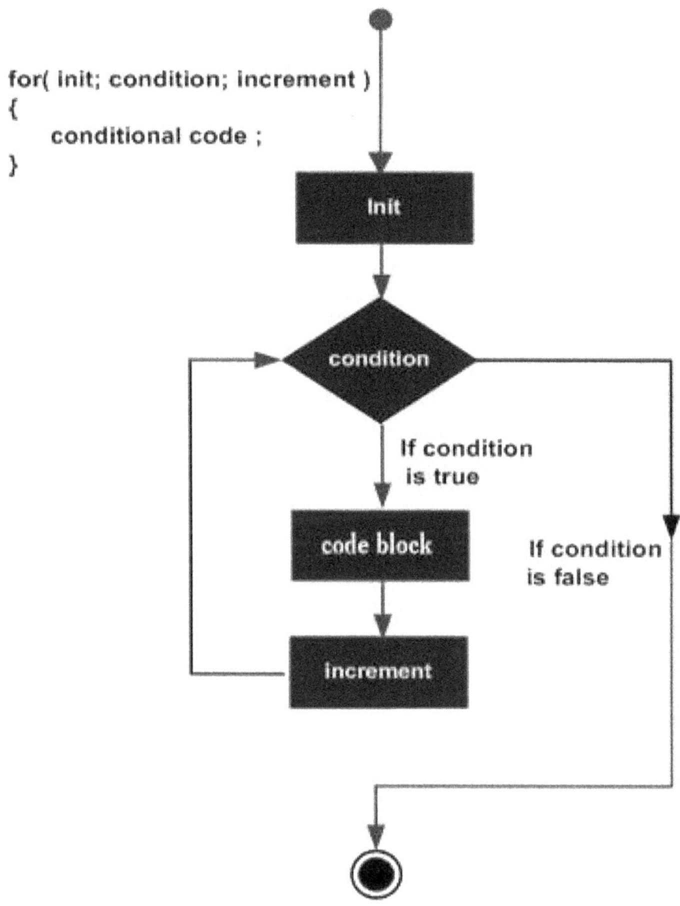

Figure 2-5 : Flow Daigram of For Loop

Example:

```
int count = 4;
for (int i = 1; i < = count; i++)
{
  MessageBox.Show("Current value of i is - " + i);
}
```

3) do...while loop:

- Unlike **for** and **while** loops, which test the loop condition at the start of the loop, the **do...while** loop checks its condition at the end of the loop.
- A **do...while** loop is similar to a while loop, except that a do...while loop is guaranteed to execute at least one time.

Syntax

```
do
{
  statement(s);

}while( condition );
```

- Notice that the conditional expression appears at the end of the loop, so the statement(s) in the loop execute once before the condition is tested.
- If the condition is true, the flow of Control jumps back up to do, and the statement(s) in the loop execute again. This process repeats until the given condition becomes false.

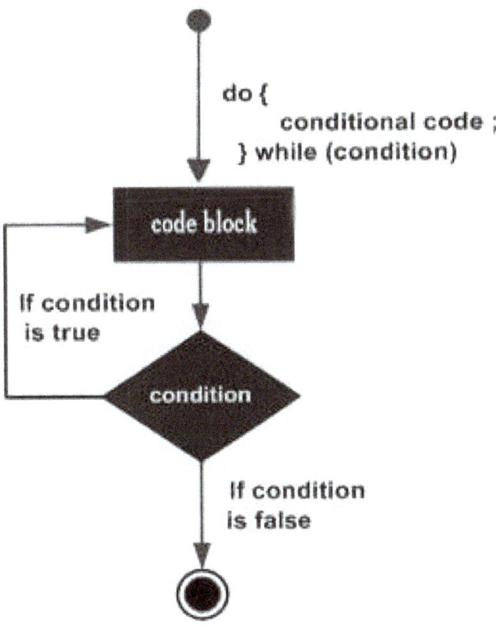

Figure 2-6 : Flow of Do.While Loop

Example:

```
int count = 4;
        do{
          MessageBox.Show(" Loop Executed ");
          count++;
        }while (count < =4);
```

• • •

2.12 Object oriented basic of C#

1. Class:

- A class is the core of any modern Object Oriented Programming language such as C#.
- In OOP languages it is mandatory to create a class for representing data.
- A class is a blueprint of an object that contains variables for storing data and functions to perform operations on the data.
- A class will not occupy any memory space and hence it is only a logical representation of data.
- To create a class, you simply use the keyword "class" followed by the class name:

```
class Employee
{
}
```

2. Object :

- Objects are the basic run-time entities of an object oriented system. They may represent a person, a place or any item that the program must handle.
- "An object is a software bundle of related variable and methods."
- **"An object is an instance of a class"**
- A class will not occupy any memory space. Hence to work with the data represented by the class you must create a variable for the class, that is called an object.
- When an object is created using the new operator, memory is allocated for the class in the heap, the object is called an instance and its starting address will be stored in the object in stack memory.
- When an object is created without the new operator, memory will not be allocated in the heap, in other words an instance will not be created

and the object in the stack contains the value null.

- When an object contains null, then it is not possible to access the members of the class using that object.

```
class Employee
{
}
```

- **Syntax to create an object of class Employee:**

```
Employee objEmp = new Employee();
```

• • •

2.13 OOPS Concepts:

- Below are some basic oops concepts:

1. Abstraction
2. Inheritance
3. Encapsulation
4. Polymorphism

1. Abstraction:

- Abstraction is "To represent the essential feature without representing the background details."
- Abstraction lets you focus on what the object does instead of how it does it.
- Abstraction provides you a generalized view of your classes or objects by providing relevant information.
- Abstraction is the process of hiding the working style of an object, and showing the information of an object in an understandable manner.

Real-world Example of Abstraction

- Suppose you have an object Mobile Phone.
- Suppose you have 3 mobile phones as in the following:
- Nokia 1400 (Features: Calling, SMS)
- Nokia 2700 (Features: Calling, SMS, FM Radio, MP3, Camera)
- Black Berry (Features:Calling, SMS, FM Radio, MP3, Camera, Video Recording, Reading Emails)
- Abstract information (necessary and common information) for the object "Mobile Phone" is that it makes a call to any number and can send SMS.

```
class MobilePhone
{
 public void Calling();
 public void SendSMS();
}
        public class Nokia1400: MobilePhone
        {
        }
        public class Nokia2700: MobilePhone
        {
        public void FMRadio();
        public void MP3();
        public void Camera();
        }
        public class BlackBerry: MobilePhone
        {
          public void FMRadio();
          public void MP3();
          public void Camera();
        public void   Recording();
        public void ReadAndSendEmails();
        }
```

- Abstraction means putting all the variables and methods in a class that are necessary.
- For example: Abstract class and abstract method.

Example

- If somebody in your collage tells you to fill in an application form, you will provide your details, like name, address, date of birth, which semester, percentage you have etcetera.
- If some doctor gives you an application to fill in the details, you will provide the details, like name, address, date of birth, blood group, height and weight.
- See in the preceding example what is in common?
- Age, name and address, so you can create a class that consists of the common data. That is called an abstract class.
- That class is not complete and it can be inherited by other classes.

2. Inheritance:

- "Defining new classes from the existing one. The new class will get all the methods and properties of the existing class."
- The new class known as sub class / child class / derived class.
- The existing class known as super class / parent class / base class.
- Inheritance is basically used for reuse the code and focus to make generic kind of thing rather than specific one.
- Inheritance is a process of object reusability.

For example, a child includes the properties of its parents.

```
public class ParentClass
{
  public ParentClass()
 {
     Console.WriteLine("Parent Constructor.");
  }
  public void print()
{
     Console.WriteLine("I'm a Parent Class.");
  }
}
public class ChildClass: ParentClass
{
   public ChildClass()
{
     Console.WriteLine("Child Constructor.");
  }
  public static void Main()
{
     ChildClass   child   =   new   ChildClass();
child.print();
  }
}
```

OUTPUT:
Parent Constructor.
Child Constructor.
I'm a Parent Class.

3. Encapsulation:

- Wrapping up a data member and a method together into a single unit (in other words class) is called Encapsulation.
- Encapsulation is like enclosing in a capsule. That is enclosing the related operations and data related to an object into that object.
- Encapsulation is like your bag in which you can keep your pen, book etcetera. It means this is the property of encapsulating members and functions.

```
class Bag
{
book;
pen;
ReadBook();
}
```

- Encapsulation means hiding the internal details of an object, in other words how an object does something.
- Encapsulation prevents clients from seeing its inside view, where the behaviour of the abstraction is implemented.
- Encapsulation is a technique used to protect the information in an object from another object.
- Hide the data for security such as making the variables private, and expose the property to access the private data that will be public.
- So, when you access the property you can validate the data and set it.

```
class Demo
{
 private int mark;
public int Mark
{
      get
{
          return _mark;
      }
set {
          if (_mark > 0) _mark = value;
else _mark = 0;
      }
  }
}
```

Real-world Example of Encapsulation

- Let's use as an example Mobile Phones and Mobile Phone Manufacturers.
- Suppose you are a Mobile Phone Manufacturer and you have designed and developed a Mobile Phone design (a class). Now by using machinery you are manufacturing Mobile Phones (objects) for selling, when you sell your Mobile Phone the user only learns how to use the Mobile Phone but not how the Mobile Phone works.
- This means that you are creating the class with functions and by with objects (capsules) of which you are making available the functionality of your class by that object and without the interference in the original class.

Example 2

- TV operation

- It is encapsulated with a cover and we can operate it with a remote and there is no need to open the TV to change the channel.
- Here everything is private except the remote, so that anyone can access the remote to operate and change the things in the TV.

4. Polymorphism :

- Polymorphism in the context of object-oriented programming, is the ability to create a variable, a function, or an object that has more than one form.
- Polymorphism means one name, many forms.
- One function behaves in different forms.
- In other words, "Many forms of a single object is called Polymorphism."

Real-world Example of Polymorphism

Example 1 A teacher behaves students.

A teacher behaves his/her seniors. Here teacher is an object but the attitude is different in different situations.

Example 2 A person behaves the son in a house at the same time that the person behaves an employee in an office.

Example 3 Your mobile phone, one name but many forms:

As phone

As camera

As mp3 player

As radio

• • •

CHAPTER III

ASP.NET Validation Controls, State Management & Navigation

3.1 Validation Control

ASP.NET Validation Controls validate the user input data to ensure that useless, unauthenticated, or contradictory data don't get stored. **ASP.NET provides the following Validation Controls:**

1. RequiredFieldValidator
2. RangeValidator
3. CompareValidator
4. RegularExpressionValidator
5. CustomValidator
6. ValidationSummary

BaseValidator Class

The ValidationControl classes are inherited from the BaseValidator class hence they inherit its properties and methods. Therefore, it would help to take a look at the properties and the methods of this base class, **which are common for all the Validation Controls:**

Members	Description
ControlToValidate	Indicates the input control to validate.
Display	Indicates how the error message is shown.
EnableClientScript	Indicates whether client side validation will take.
Enabled	Enables or disables the validator.
ErrorMessage	Indicates error string.
Text	Error text to be shown if validation fails.
IsValid	Indicates whether the value of the control is valid.
SetFocusOnError	It indicates whether in case of an invalid control, the focus should switch to the related input control.
ValidationGroup	The logical group of multiple validators, where this control belongs.
Validate()	This method revalidates the control and updates the IsValid property.

Table 3-1 : Validation Controls

1. *RequiredFieldValidator :*

The RequiredFieldValidator control ensures that the required field is not empty. It is generally tied to a text box to force input into the text box.

The syntax of the control is as given:

<asp:RequiredFieldValidator ID="rfvcandidate" runat="server" ControlToValidate ="ddlcandidate" ErrorMessage="Please choose a candidate" InitialValue="Please choose a candidate"> </asp:RequiredFieldValidator>

2. *RangeValidator :*

The RangeValidator control verifies that the input value falls within a predetermined range.

It has three specific properties:

Properties	Description
Type	It defines the type of the data. The available values are: Currency, Date, Double, Integer, and String.
MinimumValue	It specifies the minimum value of the range.
MaximumValue	It specifies the maximum value of the range.

Table 3-2 : RangeValidator Properties

The syntax of the control is as given :

<asp:RangeValidator ID="rvclass" runat="server" ControlToValidate="txtclass" ErrorMessage="Enter your class (6 - 12)" MaximumValue="12" MinimumValue="6" Type="Integer"></asp:RangeValidator>

3. CompareValidator :

The CompareValidator control compares a value in one control with a fixed value or a value in another control.

It has the following specific properties:

Properties	Description
Type	It specifies the data type.
ControlToCompare	It specifies the value of the input control to compare with.
ValueToCompare	It specifies the constant value to compare with.
Operator	It specifies the comparison operator, the available values are: Equal, NotEqual, GreaterThan, GreaterThanEqual, LessThan, LessThanEqual, and DataTypeCheck.

Table 3-3 : CompareValidator Properties

The basic syntax of the control is as follows:

<asp:CompareValidator ID="CompareValidator1" runat="server" ErrorMessage="CompareValidator"> </asp:CompareValidator>

4. RegularExpressionValidator :

The RegularExpressionValidator allows validating the input text by matching against a pattern of a regular expression. The regular expression is set in the ValidationExpression property.

The following table summarizes the commonly used syntax constructs for regular expressions:

Character Escapes	Description
\b	Matches a backspace.
\t	Matches a tab.
\r	Matches a carriage return.
\v	Matches a vertical tab.
\f	Matches a form feed.
\n	Matches a new line.
\	Escape character.

Table 3-4 :Regular Expressions

Apart from single character match, a class of characters could be specified that can be matched, called the metacharacters.

Metacharacters	Description
.	Matches any character except \n.
[abcd]	Matches any character in the set.
[^abcd]	Excludes any character in the set.
[2-7a-mA-M]	Matches any character specified in the range.
\w	Matches any alphanumeric character and underscore.
\W	Matches any non-word character.
\s	Matches whitespace characters like, space, tab, new line etc.
\S	Matches any non-whitespace character.
\d	Matches any decimal character.
\D	Matches any non-decimal character.

Table 3-5 : Metacharacters

Quantifiers could be added to specify number of times a character could appear.

Quantifier	Description
*	Zero or more matches.
+	One or more matches.
?	Zero or one matches.
{N}	N matches.
{N,}	N or more matches.
{N,M}	Between N and M matches.

Table 3-6 : Quantifier

The syntax of the control is as given

```
<asp:RegularExpressionValidator ID="string" runat="server"
ErrorMessage="string"
ValidationExpression="string" ValidationGroup="string">
</asp:RegularExpressionValidator>
```

5. CustomValidator :

The CustomValidator control allows writing application specific custom validation routines for both the client side and the server side validation.

The client side validation is accomplished through the ClientValidationFunction property. The client side validation routine should be written in a scripting language, such as JavaScript or VBScript, which the browser can understand.

The server side validation routine must be called from the control's ServerValidate event handler.The server side validation routine should be written in any .Net language, like C# or VB.Net.

The basic syntax for the control is as given

```
<asp:CustomValidator ID="CustomValidator1 "runat="server"
ClientValidationFunction=.cvf_func. ErrorMessage="CustomValidator">
</asp:CustomValidator>
```

6. ValidationSummary :

The ValidationSummary control does not perform any validation but shows a summary of all errors in the page. The summary displays the values of the ErrorMessage property of all validation controls that failed validation

The following two mutually inclusive properties list out the error message:

- **1. ShowSummary** : shows the error messages in specified format.
- **2. ShowMessageBox** : shows the error messages in a separate window

The syntax for the control is as given:

```
<asp:ValidationSummary ID="ValidationSummary1" runat="server"
DisplayMode = "BulletList" ShowSummary = "true"
HeaderText="Errors:" />
```

• • •

3.2 State Management

State management is essential to any Web application, because every Web application has information that needs to application has information that needs to be preserved from age to page.

Two Types:

1. **Client Based**

- View state
- Query strings
- Cookies
- Control state
- Hidden fields

2. Sever Based

- Application State
- Sassion State

Why state is required?

- The majority of Internet applications operate using the HTTP protocol.
- HTTP is stateless, this means that each request for a page is treated as a new request by the server.
- As a result, information from one request is generally not available to the next request..
- For this reason, most server side technologies include some mechanism for managing and preserving state.

1. Client Based

1) View State:

- The view state is the state of the page and all its controls. It is automatically maintained across posts by the ASP.NET framework.
- When a page is sent back to the client, the changes in the properties of the page and its controls are determined, and stored in the value of a hidden input field named _VIEWSTATE. When the page is again posted back, the _VIEWSTATE field is sent to the server with the HTTP request.

The view state could be enabled or disabled for:

- The entire application by setting the EnableViewState property in the <pages> section of web.config file.
- A page by setting the EnableViewState attribute of the Page directive, as

```
<%@ Page Language="C#" EnableViewState="false" %>
```

- A control by setting the Control.EnableViewState property.

Example

The following example demonstrates the concept of storing view state. Let us keep a counter, which is incremented each time the page is posted back by clicking a button on the page. A label control shows the value in the counter.

The markup file code is as follows:

```
<%@ Page Language="C#" AutoEventWireup="true" CodeBehind="Default.aspx.cs" Inherits
    ="statedemo._Default" %>

<!DOCTYPE html PUBLIC "-//W3C//DTD XHTML 1.0 Transitional//EN" "http://www.w3.org/TR/xhtml1
    /DTD/xhtml1-transitional.dtd">

<html xmlns="http://www.w3.org/1999/xhtml" >

   <head runat="server">
      <title>
         Untitled Page
      </title>
   </head>

   <body>
      <form id="form1" runat="server">

         <div>
            <h3>View State demo</h3>

            Page Counter:

            <asp:Label ID="lblCounter" runat="server" />
            <asp:Button ID="btnIncrement" runat="server" Text="Add Count" onclick
               ="btnIncrement_Click" />
         </div>

      </form>
   </body>
```

The code behind file for the example is shown here:

```
public partial class _Default : System.Web.UI.Page
{
   public int counter
   {
      get
      {
         if (ViewState["pcounter"] != null)
         {
            return ((int)ViewState["pcounter"]);
         }
         else
         {
            return 0;
         }
      }

      set
      {
         ViewState["pcounter"] = value;
      }
   }

   protected void Page_Load(object sender, EventArgs e)
   {
      lblCounter.Text = counter.ToString();
      counter++;
   }
}
```

It would produce the following result:

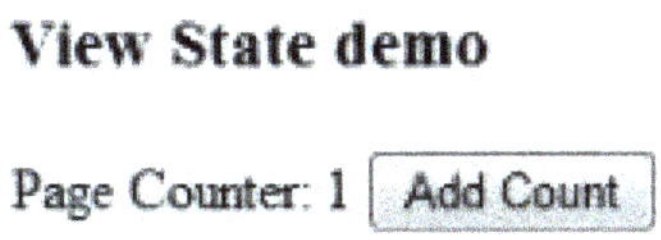

View State demo

Page Counter: 1 [Add Count]

2) Query Strings :

- A querystring can be used to submit data back to the same page or to another page through the URL.
- It is a format that is used to transfer values from one page to other page. Whenever form is submitted the values are posted to server by browser using query string format only.
- Format is<program name>?<name>=<value>&<name>=<value>....

Example:

```
demo.aspx?a=10&b=20
```

Example 1:

```
Response.write(Request["Textbox1"])
```

This is to get a textbox value in same form.

Example 2:

In first form (calling form)

```
Response.Redirect("view.aspx?a=" +Textbox1.text);
```

In second form (called form)

```
Label1.text=Request["a"];
```

3) Cookies :

- Cookies are a client-side approach for persisting state information.
- They are name-value pairs that are saved within one or more files that are managed by the browser.
- These pairs accompany both server requests and responses within the HTTP header.

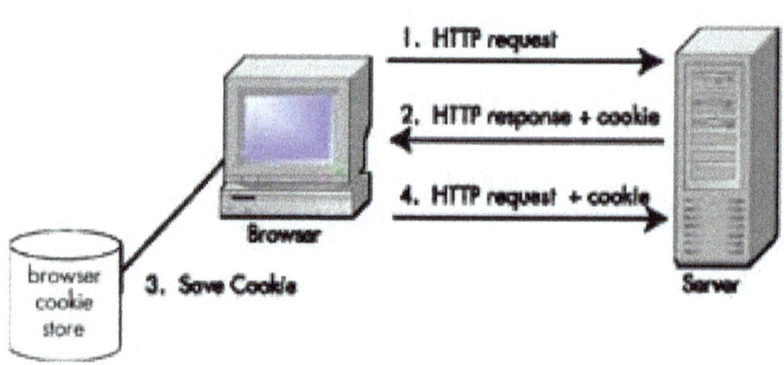

- Although cookies can be used for any state-related purpose, they are principally used as a way of maintaining continuity over time in a Web application over time in a Web application.
- One typical use of cookies in a Web site is to "remember" the visitor, so that the server can customize the site for the user. Some sites use cookies as part of their shopping cart implementation so that items added to the cart remain there even if the user leaves the site and then comes back. user leaves the site and then comes back.

For creating cookies using ASP.NET we have two options:
1. Using Response.Cookies collection
2. Using HttpCookie class of .NET

- **Example:**

Using cookie for creating and reading in memory cookies

- **To create cookie we write following code in Button_click event**

```
HttpCookie x= new HttpCookie("user"); x.Value= Textbox1.Text;
Response.Cookie.Add(x);
Repsonse.Write("Information stored");
```

- **To read cookie and display the value in label, we write following code in Page_Load event**

```
if(Request.Cookies["user"] != null)
Label1.Text = Request.Cookies["user"].Value;
else
Label1.Text = "No Data";
```

4) Hidden fields :

- It is used to store normal data during post backs. As it is hidden field, it is not visible at the browser though it is rendered as simple HTML filed.

- It is available only when the page is submitted using HTTP POST command.

Example:

we see how hidden filed value can be retrieved on postback.

<input type="hidden" id="Message" value="Hello" runat="server" />

When page is rendered, the hidden field control is rendered in html form like this:

<input name="ctl00$ContentPlaceHolder1$Message" type="hidden" id="ctl00_ContentPlaceHolder_Message" value="Hello" />

Now, Create following button

Show Message

For this we have to write Button_Click event like this:

Button1.Text=Messge.value;

When button clicked, the value in hidden field is read and assigned to the button text which is displayed when the page is posted back as below:

Hello..how r u?

5) Control State :

- Control state cannot be modified, accessed directly, or disabled.

2) Server Based

I. Application State :

- When a user connects to an ASP.NET website, a new session object is created. When session state is turned on, a new session state object is created for each new request. This session state object becomes part of the context and it is available through the page.
- Session state is generally used for storing application data such as inventory, supplier list, customer record, or shopping cart. It can also keep information about the user and his preferences, and keep the track of pending operations.

The HttpApplicationState class has the following properties:

Properties	Description
Item(name)	The value of the application state item with the specified name. This is the default property of the HttpApplicationState class.
Count	The number of items in the application state collection.

Table 3-7 : HttpApplicationState Propertites

The HttpApplicationState class has the following methods:

Methods	Description
Add(name, value)	Adds an item to the application state collection.
Clear	Removes all the items from the application state collection.
Remove(name)	Removes the specified item from the application state collection.
RemoveAll	Removes all objects from an HttpApplicationState collection.
RemoveAt	Removes an HttpApplicationState object from a collection by index.
Lock()	Locks the application state collection so only the current user can access it.
Unlock()	Unlocks the application state collection so all the users can access it.

Table 3-8 : HttpApplicationState Methods

- Application state data is generally maintained by writing handlers for the events:

  Application_Start
  Application_End
  Application_Error
  Session_Start
  Session_End

- The following code snippet shows the basic syntax for storing application state information:

```
Void Application_Start(object sender, EventArgs e)
{
   Application["startMessage"] = "The application has started.";
}

Void Application_End(object sender, EventArgs e)
{
   Application["endtMessage"] = "The application has ended.";
}
```

II. Server State :

- When a user connects to an ASP.NET website, a new session object is created. When session state is turned on, a new session state object is created for each new request. This session state object becomes part of the context and it is available through the page.
- Session state is generally used for storing application data such as inventory, supplier list, customer record, or shopping cart. It can also keep information about the user and his preferences, and keep the track of pending operations.

- Sessions are identified and tracked with a 120-bit SessionID, which is passed from client to server and back as cookie or a modified URL. The SessionID is globally unique and random.
- The session state object is created from the HttpSessionState class, which defines a collection of session state items.

The HttpSessionState class has the following properties:

Properties	Description
SessionID	The unique session identifier.
Item(name)	The value of the session state item with the specified name. This is the default property of the HttpSessionState class.
Count	The number of items in the session state collection.
TimeOut	Gets and sets the amount of time, in minutes, allowed between requests before the session-state provider terminates the session.

Table 3-9 : HttpSessionState Class Properties

The HttpSessionState class has the following methods:

Methods	Description
Add(name, value)	Adds an item to the application state collection.
Clear	Removes all the items from the application state collection.
Remove(name)	Removes the specified item from the application state collection.
RemoveAll	Removes all objects from an HttpApplicationState collection.
RemoveAt	Removes an HttpApplicationState object from a collection by index.
Lock()	Locks the application state collection so only the current user can access it.
Unlock()	Unlocks the application state collection so all the users can access it.

Table 3-10 : HttpSessionState Class Methods

The session state object is a name-value pair to store and retrieve some information from the session state object. You could use the following code for the same:

```
void StoreSessionInfo()
{
   String fromuser = TextBox1.Text;
   Session["fromuser"] = fromuser;
}

void RetrieveSessionInfo()
{
   String fromuser = Session["fromuser"];
   Label1.Text = fromuser;
}
```

The above code stores only strings in the Session dictionary object, however, it can store all the primitive data types and arrays composed of primitive data types, as well as the DataSet, DataTable, HashTable, and Image objects, as well as any user-defined class that inherits from the ISerializable object.

Example

The following example demonstrates the concept of storing session state. There are two buttons on the page, a text box to enter string and a label to display the text stored from last session.

The mark up file code is as follows:

```
<%@ Page Language="C#" AutoEventWireup="true"  CodeFile="Default.aspx.cs" Inherits
    ="_Default"  %>

<!DOCTYPE html PUBLIC "-//W3C//DTD XHTML 1.0 Transitional//EN" "http://www.w3.org/TR
    /xhtml1/DTD/xhtml1-transitional.dtd">

<html xmlns="http://www.w3.org/1999/xhtml" >

   <head runat="server">
      <title>
         Untitled Page
      </title>
   </head>

   <body>
      <form id="form1" runat="server">
         <div>
                 

            <table style="width: 568px; height: 103px">

               <tr>
                  <td style="width: 209px">
                     <asp:Label ID="lblstr" runat="server" Text="Enter a String"  style
                        ="width:94px">
                     </asp:Label>
                  </td>
```

```
    <td style="width: 317px">
        <asp:TextBox ID="txtstr" runat="server" style="width:227px">
        </asp:TextBox>
    </td>
</tr>

<tr>
    <td style="width: 209px"> </td>
    <td style="width: 317px"> </td>
</tr>

<tr>
    <td style="width: 209px">
        <asp:Button ID="btnnrm" runat="server"
            Text="No action button" style="width:128px" />
    </td>

    <td style="width: 317px">
        <asp:Button ID="btnstr" runat="server"
            OnClick="btnstr_Click" Text="Submit the String" />
    </td>
</tr>

<tr>
    <td style="width: 209px">  </td>

    <td style="width: 317px">  </td>
</tr>
```

```
            <tr>
                <td style="width: 209px">
                    <asp:Label ID="lblsession" runat="server"  style="wid
                    </asp:Label>
                </td>

                <td style="width: 317px">  </td>
            </tr>

            <tr>
                <td style="width: 209px">
                    <asp:Label ID="lblshstr" runat="server">
                    </asp:Label>
                </td>

                <td style="width: 317px">  </td>
            </tr>

        </table>
    </div>
  </form>
</body>
```

It should look like the following in design view:

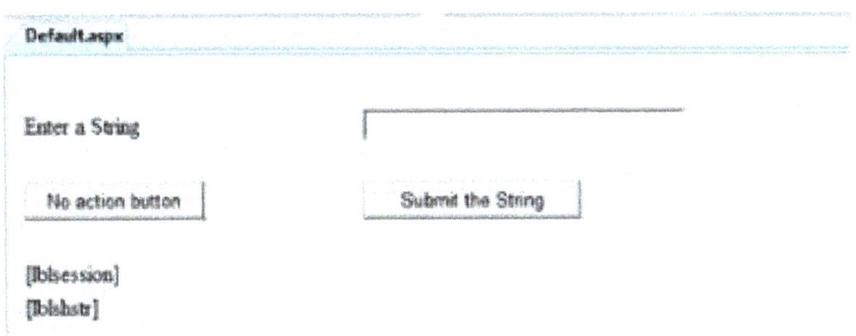

The code behind file is given here:

```
public partial class _Default : System.Web.UI.Page
{
    String mystr;

    protected void Page_Load(object sender, EventArgs e)
    {
        this.lblshstr.Text = this.mystr;
        this.lblsession.Text = (String)this.Session["str"];
    }

    protected void btnstr_Click(object sender, EventArgs e)
    {
        this.mystr = this.txtstr.Text;
        this.Session["str"] = this.txtstr.Text;
        this.lblshstr.Text = this.mystr;
        this.lblsession.Text = (String)this.Session["str"];
    }
}
```

Execute the file and observe how it works:

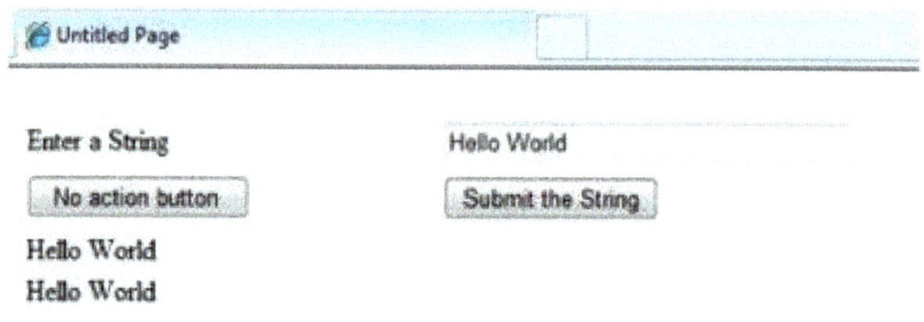

• • •

3.3 Master Page

- Master Pages are a template that other pages can inherit from to keep consistent functionality.

- The pages that inherit from Master Pages are referred to as content pages.

Master Pages are architected with a merging concept. A content page refers to a Master Page and the ASP.NET framework merges the two pages together to make one page.

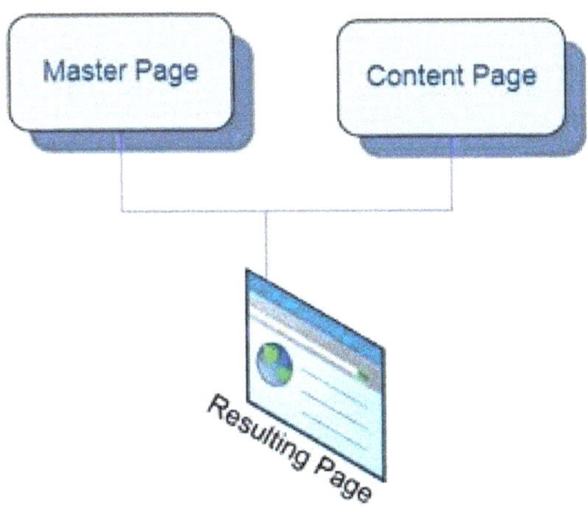

- It contains the extension .master.
- It has a Master Page directive at the top of the page:

<%@Master language="C#"%>.

This replaces the more typical <%@ Page directive that you will see on most ASP. NET Pages.

- The difference between a Master Page and regular ASP.NET is that the Master Page can have special sections called ContentPlaceHolders. A ContentPlaceHolder is a place holder section that the content pages can fill in for the Master Page.

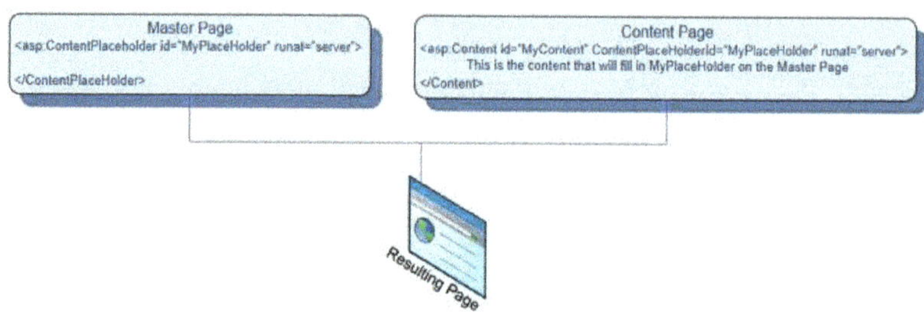

ASP.NET Master Page :

```
<html id="HTML1" runat="server" xmlns:o="urn:schemas-microsoft-com:office:office">
        <head id="HEAD1" runat="server">
                <META Name="GENERATOR" Content="Microsoft SharePoint">
                <META Name="progid" Content="SharePoint.WebPartPage.Document">
                <META HTTP-EQUIV="Content-Type" CONTENT="text/html; charset=utf-8">
                <META HTTP-EQUIV="Expires" content="0">
                <link rel="stylesheet" type="text/css" href="/_layouts/1033/styles/core.css" />
        </head>
        <body>
         <form id="Form1" runat="server" >
                <div>
                        Hello
                </div>
              <asp:ContentPlaceHolder id="MyPlaceHolder" runat="server">

              </asp:ContentPlaceHolder>

                ...
```

If the ContentPlaceHolder of a Master Page is empty, it will be filled in by the implementing content page. Alternatively , the ContentPlaceHolder can have Web code inside of it, which will be used if implementing content page does not implement the particular ContentPlaceHolder.

Content Pages :

Content pages are the ASP.NET pages that implement a Master Page. Content pages are normal ASP.NET pages that contain an attribute which informs the compiler that the pages should be merged with a Master Page. This attribute is part of the page directive tag and is called the MasterPageFile.

<%@ Page Language="C#" AutoEventWireup="true" MasterPageFile="~/Site1.Master" CodeBehind="Default.aspx.cs" Inherits="WebApplication1._Default" %>

Content pages contain content tags. Content tags let the compiler know which ContentPlaceHolders to override the Master Page.

<asp:Content ID="MyContent" ContentPlaceHolderId="MyPlaceHolder" runat ="server">

This is the content that will override the ContentPlaceHolder "MyPlaceHolder" from the

Master Page </asp:Content>

Example:

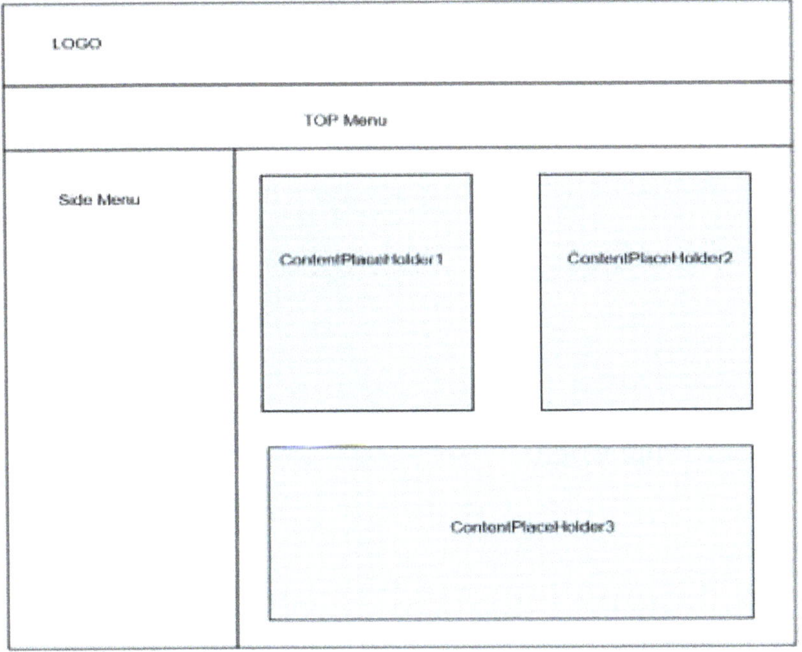

Master Page Code :

```
<%@ Master Language="C#" AutoEventWireup="true" CodeBehind="Site1.master.cs"
Inherits="WebApplication1.Site1" %>

<!DOCTYPE html PUBLIC "-//W3C//DTD XHTML 1.0 Transitional//EN"
"http://www.w3.org/TR/xhtml1/DTD/xhtml1-transitional.dtd">

<html xmlns="http://www.w3.org/1999/xhtml" >
<head runat="server">
    <title>Untitled Page</title>
</head>
<body>
    <form id="form1" runat="server" style="width: 1200px" >
        <div style="border:solid 1px">
            Logo
        </div>
        <div style="border:solid 1px">
            Top Menu
        </div>
        <div style="width:300px;  height: 286px;float:left;border:solid 1px">
            Side Menu
        </div>
        <div style="border:solid 1px; height: 286px;">
            <div style="border:solid 1px; height: 124px; width: 400px;float:left; margin:10px">
                <asp:ContentPlaceHolder ID="ContentPlaceHolder1" runat="server">

                </asp:ContentPlaceHolder>
            </div>
            <div style="border:solid 1px; height: 124px; width: 400px; margin:10px">
                <asp:ContentPlaceHolder ID="ContentPlaceHolder2" runat="server">

               </asp:ContentPlaceHolder>
            </div>
            <div style="border:solid 1px; height: 124px; width:812px; margin:10px">
                <asp:ContentPlaceHolder ID="ContentPlaceHolder3" runat="server">

               </asp:ContentPlaceHolder>
            </div>

        </div>

    </form>
</body>
</html>
```

Content Page Code:

```
<%@ Page Language="C#" AutoEventWireup="true" MasterPageFile="~/Site1.Master"
CodeBehind="Default.aspx.cs" Inherits="WebApplication1._Default" %>

<asp:Content ID="Content1" ContentPlaceHolderId="ContentPlaceHolder1" runat="server">
      This is the content that will override the ContentPlaceHolder "ContentPlaceHolder1" from
the Master Page
</asp:Content>

<asp:Content ID="Content3" ContentPlaceHolderId="ContentPlaceHolder3" runat="server">
      This is the content that will override the ContentPlaceHolder "ContentPlaceHolder3" from
the Master Page
</asp:Content>

<asp:Content ID="Content2" ContentPlaceHolderId="ContentPlaceHolder2" runat="server">
      This is the content that will override the ContentPlaceHolder "ContentPlaceHolder2" from
the Master Page
</asp:Content>
```

• • •

3.4 Navigation

- Navigation control in ASP.NET manages the data passing between ASPX pages. Web applications are having multiple pages interconnected with each other. So proper navigation system must be there which can help the end user to successfully work through an application.
- There are standard methods are available in ASP.NET 1.x that offers well defined navigation system for the web application. Only the method which is present for building navigation within web application is to fill the pages with hyperlinks. The drawbacks of hyperlink are when you move pages around or change pages names.
- **Different Navigation Controls in ASP.NET:**

  1. SiteMapPath
  2. Menu Control
  3. TreeView

1. SiteMapPath Control :

- Site maps are XML files which are mainly used to describe the logical structure of the web application. It defines the layout of all pages in web application and how they relate to each other.
- Whenever you want you can add or remove pages to your site map there by managing navigation of website efficiently.
- Site map files are defined with .sitemap extension. <sitemap> element is the root node of the sitemap file.
- It has three attributes:

1. **Title:** It provides textual description of the link.
2. **URL:** It provides the location of the valid physical file.
3. **Description:** It is used for tooltip of the link.

- SiteMapPath control displays the navigation path of the current page. The path acts as click able links to previous page.
- The sitemap path control uses the web. This control creates the navigation mechanism which is linear path defining where the user is currently located in navigation arrangement.
- It helps end user to know his location in relation to the rest of the site.

Properties of SiteMapPath Control:

1. **PathSeparator :** This property is to get or set the out separator text.
2. **NodeStyle :** This property is used to set the style of all nodes that will be displayed.
3. **RootNodeStyle :** This property is used to set the style on the absolute root node.
4. **PathDirection :** This property is used to set the direction of the links generated in the output.
5. **CurrentNodeStyle :** This property is used to set the style on node that represent the current page.
6. **ShowToolTips :** This property is used to set the tooltip for the control. Default value is true.
7. **PathSeparatorStyle :** This property ja used to set the style of path separator.

2. Menu Control :

- Menu is an another navigation control in ASP.NET which is used to display menu in web page. This control is used in combination with SiteMapDataSource control for navigating the web Site.
- It displays two types of menu static menu and dynamic menu. Static menu is always displayed in menu Control, by default only menu items at the root levels are displayed.
- Dynamic menu is displayed only when the use moves the mouse pointer over the parent menu that contains a dynamic sub menu.

Properties of Menu Control:

1. **DataSourceID** : This property is used to specify the data source to be used using sitemap file as data source.
2. **CssClass** : This property is used to specify the CSS class attribute for the control.
3. **ImgeUrl** : This property is used to specify the image that appear next to the menu item.
4. **Orientation** : This property is used to specify the alignment of menu control. It can be horizontal or vertical.
5. **Tooltip** : This property is used to specify the tooltip of the menu item when you mouse over.
6. **Text** : This property is used to specify the text to display in the menu.
7. **NavigateUrl** : This property is used to specify the target location to send the user when menu item is clicked.
8. **Target** : This property is used to specify the target page location. It can be in new window or same window.
9. **Value** : This property is used to specify the unique id to use in server side events.

3. Tree View :

- TreeView is an another navigation control used in ASP.NET to display the data in hierarchical list manner. When TreeView is displayed for the first time, it displays all of its nodes.
- User can control it by setting the property called ExpandDepth.

Properties of TreeView Control:

1. **DataSourceID** : This property is used to specify the data source to be used using sitemap file s data source.
2. **ShowLines** : This property is used to specify the lines to connect the individual item in the tree.
3. **CssClass** : This property is used to specify the CSS class attribute for the control.
4. **ExpandDepth** : This property is used to specify the level at which items in the tree are expanded.

CHAPTER IV

Data Access through ADO.NET

4.1 ADO.NET :

- ADO.NET refers to the various classes in the .NET Framework that provide data access.
- ADO.NET is typically used to access relational databases.
- It can also be used to access other external data such as XML documents data such as XML documents.

ADO.NET Architecture:

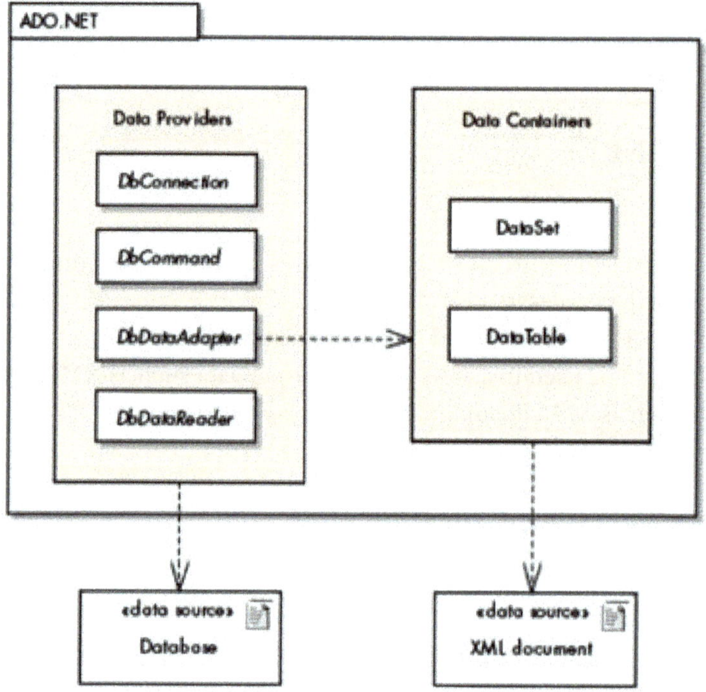

Figure 4-1 : ADO.NET Architecture

ADO.NET Data Providers:

The ADO.NET data providers are a handful of .NET classes that are used for:

- connecting to a database
- executing data commands
- populating DataSet
- providing fast, forward only, read only access to data.

The four main classes within a data provider are

- DbConnection

- DbCommand
- DbDataAdpater
- DbDataReader

The key point about .NET data providers is each database type has its own version of these classes. Because DbConnection, DbCommand, DbDataAdapter, and DbDataReader are abstract classes each provider are abstract classes, each provider implements its own concrete version of these classes.

- SqlConnection class defined in the SQLServer data provider.
- OracleConnection class defined in the Oracle data provider.

ADO.NET Namespaces:

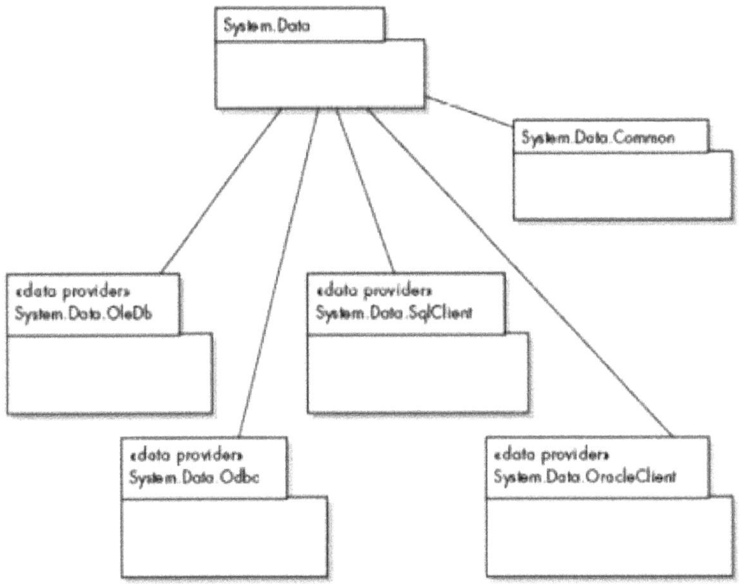

Figure 2 : ADO.NET Namespace

Abstract base classes for Data Provider:

Class	Description
DbCommand	Executes a data Command. Such as a SQL Statement or a Store Procedure
DbConnection	Establishes a connection to a Data Source.
DbDataAdapter	Populates a Dataset from a data source.
DbDataReader	Represents a read-only, forward-only stream of data from a data source.

Table 4-1 Abstract base classes for Data Provider

Using Data Provider Classes:

The process for using these classes is as follows:

1. Create a DbConnection to the database via a connection string.
2. Create and execute a DbCommand for the database.

Fill a DataSet from the database using a DbDataAdpater, or use a DbdataReader to retrieve data from database.

1) Data Connection:

Represents a connection to a data source through which commands are passed to the data source and through which data is returned returned.

- Before you can access a database, you must first create a connection to it.
- Database commands then "travel" across the connection to the database, as does any data returned from a database.
- Each DbConnection class has members for:

  - Opening and closing connection
  - setting and retrieving properties of connection
  - handling connection related events

Connection String:

To create a connection, you must specify a connection string.

- A connection string is a string that specifies the initialization and connection information needed to connect to a data source.
- It can contain information such as the database name or location, driver type, user name, password, and even connection pooling and timeout information.

Syntax :

```
// Must use @ since string contains backslash characters
string connString = @"Provider=Microsoft.Jet.OLEDB.4.0;Data Source=c:\data\abc.mdb;"

OleDbConnection conn = new OleDbConnection(connString);
conn.Open();

// Now use the connection
...
// all finished, so close connection
conn.Close();
```

```
string conString=("Data Source=hp;Initial Catalog=ims;Persist Security Info=True;User ID=sa;Password=***");
sqlConnection con= new sqlConnection(conString);
```

Storing Connection Strings:

You can define connection strings for your application in the Web.config file.

Web.config file

```
<configuration>
    <connectionStrings>
       <add name="Books" connectionString="Provider=..." />
       <add name="Sales" connectionString="Data Source=..." />
    </connectionStrings>
    <system.web>
    ...
    </system.web>
</configuration>
```

.aspx file:

```
string connString = WebConfigurationManager.ConnectionStrings["Books"].ConnectionString;
```

2) DbCommand:

It represents an SQL statement or a stored procedure that is executed by the data source.

- Each DbCommand class has members for:
    - representing an SQL statement
    - creating data parameters
    - executing SQL commands that either return data (Ex. SELECT) or do not return data (Ex. INSERT, DELETE & UPDATE).
    - It can be used to run stored procedures if the database supports them.

- To create a command, you instantiate the relevant DbCommand object and pass it your database DbConnection object.
- This DbConnection can be set via the constructor or via DbConnection property of the DbCommand.

- The DbCommand object also needs a database command contained in a string.

  Syntax:

```
string conString=("Data Source=hp;Initial Catalog=ims;Persist Security Info=True;User
ID=sa;Password=***"); sqlConnection con= new sqlConnection(conString);
sqlCommand cmd= new sqlCommand("SELECT * FROM Table1", con);
```

Executing a DbCommand:

Once a DbCommand object has been instantiated and its command text, command type, and connection set, the command can be run by calling one of the command can be run by calling one of the Execute methods of the DbCommand class:

- **ExecuteNonQuery:** For commands that do not return any record data, such as an SQL INSERT or DELETE.
- **ExecuteScaler:** For SELECT command that return a single value.
- **ExecuteReader:** For SELECT command that return multiple results

3) DbDataReader:

The DbDataReader is optimized for the fast retrieval of a read-only stream of records and is thus ideal for web applications.

DbDataReader is not a data container like the DataSet, but a kind of pointer to a record in a result set (that is a set of a record in a result set (that is, a set of records returned from a database query).

Programming a DbDatareader: DbDataReader objects are not created using the C# new operator.

Syntax:

```
string connString = "..."
OleDbConnection conn = new OleDbConnection(connString);

string cmdString = "SELECT Id,ProductName,Price From Products";
OleDbCommand cmd = new OleDbCommand(cmdString, conn);

conn.Open();
OleDBDataReader reader = cmd.ExecuteReader();

someControl.DataSource = reader;
someControl.DataBind();

reader.Close();
conn.Close();
```

4) DbDataAdapter: *These classes represent a bridge between the DataSet container and an underlying database.*

Each DbDataAdapter class provides a:

- Fill method for filling a DataSet (or just a DataTable) with data from the database
- Update method for outputting any changes made to the data in the DataSet back to the database.
- The DbDataAdapter can also persist changes made to the in-memory data by writing the changes back to the database.

Programming a DbAdapter:

```
DataSet ds = new DataSet();

// create a connection
SqlConnection conn = new SqlConnection(connString);

string sql = "SELECT Isbn,Title,Price FROM Books";
SqlDataAdapter adapter = new SqlDataAdapter(sql, conn);

try
{
   // read data into DataSet
   adapter.Fill(ds);

   // use the filled DataSet
}
catch (Exception ex)
{
   // process exception
}
```

Data Source Controls: There are five data source controls that come with ASP.NET.

1. **AccessDataSource:** Provides simplified access to Microsoft Access Database.
2. **SqlDataSource:** Provides access to any databases that uses SQL.
3. **ObjectDataSource:** Allows you to user your own custom class to access data.
4. **SiteMapDataSource:** Used by the site navigation controls to access the XML based site map file.
5. **XmlDataSource:** Provides access to any XML documents.

Using DataSource Controls:

Example:

```
<asp:SqlDataSource ID="dsArt" runat="server"
   ConnectionString="<%$ ConnectionStrings:Books %>"
   ProviderName="System.Data.SqlClient"
   SelectCommand="Select AuthorId,AuthorName From Authors" />

<asp:DropDownList ID="drpAuthors" runat="server"
   DataSourceID="dsArt" DataTextField="AuthorName" />
```

• • •

4.2 Gridview

- Gridview control is the successor to the DataGrid and extends it in a number of ways. With this GridView control, you could display an entire collection of data, easily add sorting and paging, and perform inline editing.
- In addition to just displaying data, the GridView can be used to edit and delete the displayed data as well.
- The DataGrid or GridView generates a BoundColumn for each field in the data source (AutoGenerateColumns=true). By directly assigning the data source to the GridView, the data can be rendered in separate columns, in the order it occurs in the data source. By default, the field names appear in the grid's column headers, and values are rendered in text labels. A default format is applied to non-string values and it can be changed.

  Behavior properties for Gridview:

AllowPaging	true/false. Indicate whether the control should support paging.
AllowSorting	true/false. Indicate whether the control should support sorting.
SortExpression	Gets the current sort expression (field name) that determines the order of the row.
SortDirection	Gets the sorting direction of the column sorted currently (Ascending/Descending).
DataSource	Gets or sets the data source object that contains the data to populate the control.
DataSourceID	Indicate the bound data source control to use (Generally used when we are using SqlDataSource or AccessDataSource to bind the data, See 1st Grid example).
AutoGenerateEditButton	true/false. Indicates whether a separate column should be added to edit the record.
AutoGenerateDeleteButton	true/false. Indicates whether a separate column should be added to delete the record.
AutoGenerateSelectButton	true/false. Indicate whether a separate column should be added to selecat a particular record.
AutoGenerateColumns	true/false. Indicate whether columns are automatically created for each field of the data source. The default is true.

Table 4-2 : Behavior properties for Gridview

State properties for Gridview:

Columns	Gets the collection of objects that represent the columns in the GridView.
EditIndex	Gets or sets the 0-based index that identifies the row currently to be edited.
FooterRow	Returns a GridViewRow object that represents the footer of the GridView.
HeaderRow	Returns a GridViewRow object that represents the header of the GridView.
PageCount	Gets the number of the pages required to display the records of the data source.
PageIndex	Gets or sets the 0-based page index.
PageIndex	Gets or sets the number of records to display in one page of GridView.
Rows	Gets a collection of GridViewRow objects that represents the currently displayed rows in the GridView.
DataKeyNames	Gets an array that contains the names of the primary key field of the currently displayed rows in the GridView.
DataKeys	Gets a collection of DataKey objects that represent the value of the primary key fields set in DataKeyNames property of the GridView.

Table 4-3 : State properties for Gridview

Different types of events:

Name	Description
DataBinding	Occurs when the server control binds to a data source. (Inherited from Control.)
DataBound	Occurs after the server control binds to a data source. (Inherited from BaseDataBoundControl.)
Disposed	Occurs when a server control is released from memory, which is the last stage of the server control lifecycle when an ASP.NET page is requested. (Inherited from Control.)
Init	Occurs when the server control is initialized, which is the first step in its lifecycle. (Inherited from Control.)
Load	Occurs when the server control is loaded into the Page object. (Inherited from Control.)
PageIndexChanged	Occurs when one of the pager buttons is clicked, but after the GridView control handles the paging operation.
PageIndexChanging	Occurs when one of the pager buttons is clicked, but before the GridView control handles the paging operation.
PreRender	Occurs after the Control object is loaded but prior to rendering. (Inherited from Control.)

RowCancelingEdit	Occurs when the Cancel button of a row in edit mode is clicked, but before the row exits edit mode.
RowCommand	Occurs when a button is clicked in a GridView control.
RowCreated	Occurs when a row is created in a GridView control.
RowDataBound	Occurs when a data row is bound to data in a GridView control.
RowDeleted	Occurs when a row's Delete button is clicked, but after the GridView control deletes the row.
RowDeleting	Occurs when a row's Delete button is clicked, but before the GridView control deletes the row.
RowEditing	Occurs when a row's Edit button is clicked, but before the GridView control enters edit mode.
RowUpdated	Occurs when a row's Update button is clicked, but after the GridView control updates the row.
RowUpdating	Occurs when a row's Update button is clicked, but before the GridView control updates the row.
SelectedIndexChanged	Occurs when a row's Select button is clicked, but after the GridView control handles the select operation.
SelectedIndexChanging	Occurs when a row's Select button is clicked, but before the GridView control handles the select operation.
Sorted	Occurs when the hyperlink to sort a column is clicked, but after the GridView control handles the sort operation.
Sorting	Occurs when the hyperlink to sort a column is clicked, but before the GridView control handles the sort operation.
Unload	Occurs when the server control is unloaded from memory. (Inherited from Control.)

Table 4-4 : Events for Gridview

• • •

4.3 Listview

- The ASP.NET Listview control enables you to bind to data items that are returned from a data source and display them. You can display data in pages. You can display items individually, or you can group them.
- The Listviewcontrol displays data in a format that you define by using templates and styles. It is useful for data in any repeating structure,

similar to the Datalist and Repeater controls. However, unlike those controls, with the Listview control you can enable users to edit, insert, and delete data, and to sort and page data, all without code.

Templates available in Listview:

The following table lists all the templates that are used with the List Viwe control.

Layout Templates

Identifies the root template that defines the main layout of the control. It contains a placeholder object, such as a table row (tr), div, or span element. This element will be replaced with the content that is defined in the ItemTemplate template or in the GroupTemplate template. It might also contain a Data Project object.

ItemTemplate

Identifies the data-bound content to display for single items.

ItemSepatatorTemplate

Identifies the content to render between single items.

GroupTemplate

Identifies the content for the group layout. It contains a placeholder object, such as a table cell (td), div, or span that will be replaced with the content defined in the other templates, such as the ItemTemplate and EmptyItemTemplate templates.

GroupSeparatorTemplate

Identifies the content to render between groups of items.

EmptyItemTemplate

Identifies the content to render for an empty item when a GroupTemplate template is used. For example, if the GroupItemCount property is set to 5, and the total number of items returned from the data source is 8, the last row of data displayed by the ListView control will contain three items as specified by the ItemTemplate template, and two items as specified by the EmptyItemtemplate template.

EmptyDataTemplate

Identifies the content to render if the data source returns no data.

SelectedItemTemplate

Identifies the content to render for the selected data item to differentiate the selected item from the other displayed items.

AlternatingItemTemplate

Identifies the content to render for alternating items to make it easier to distinguish between consecutive items.

EditItemTemplate

Identifies the content to render when an item is being edited. The EditItemTemplate template is rendered in place of the ItemTemplate template for the data item being edited.

InsertItemTemplate

Identifies the content to render when an item is being inserted. The InsertItemTemplate template is rendered in place of an ItemTemplate template at either the start of the items displayed by the ListView control, or at the end. You can specify where the InsertItemTemplate template is rendered by using the InsertItemPosition property of the ListView control.

Methods:

DataBind()	Binds a data source to the invoked server control and all its child controls.(Inherited from BaseDataBoundControl.)
OnInit(EventArgs)	Raises the Init event.(Overrides BaseDataBoundControl.OnInit(EventArgs).)
OnItemCanceling(ListViewCancelEventArgs)	Raises the ItemCanceling event.
OnItemCommand(ListViewCommandEventArgs)	Raises the ItemCommand event.
OnItemCreated(ListViewItemEventArgs)	Raises the ItemCreated event.
OnItemDataBound(ListViewItemEventArgs)	Raises the ItemDataBound event.
OnItemDeleted(ListViewDeletedEventArgs)	Raises the ItemDeleted event.
OnItemDeleting(ListViewDeleteEventArgs)	Raises the ItemDeleting event.
OnItemEditing(ListViewEditEventArgs)	Raises the ItemEditing event.
OnItemInserted(ListViewInsertedEventArgs)	Raises the ItemInserted event.
OnItemInserting(ListViewInsertEventArgs)	Raises the ItemInserting event.
OnItemUpdated(ListViewUpdatedEventArgs)	Raises the ItemUpdated event.
OnItemUpdating(ListViewUpdateEventArgs)	Raises the ItemUpdating event.

Table 4-5 : Mathods for Listview

• • •

4.4 DeatilsView Control

- DetailsView control is a data-bound control that renders a single record at a time. It can provide navigation option also. It can insert, update and delete the record also. When it is rendered on the page, generally it is implemented through <table> HTML tag.
- Its properties like BackColor, ForeColor, BorderColor, BorderStyle, BorderWidth, Height etc. are implemented through style properites of <tahle> tag.

Following are some important properties that are very useful.

Behavior Properties of the DetailsView Control	
AllowPaging	true/false. Indicate whether the control should support navigation.
DataSource	Gets or sets the data source object that contains the data to populate the control.
DataSourceID	Indicate the bound data source control to use (Generally used when we are using SqlDataSource or AccessDataSource to bind the data. See 1st Grid example).
AutoGenerateEditButton	true/false. Indicates whether a separate column with edit link/button should be added to edit the record.
AutoGenerateDeleteButton	true/false. Indicates whether a separate column with delete link/button should be added to delete the record.
AutoGenerateRows	true/false. Indicate whether rows are automatically created for each field of the data source. The default is true.
DefaultMode	read-only/insert/edit. Indicate the default display mode.

Table 4-6 : Behavior Properties for DetailsView control

Style Properties of the DetailsView Control	
AlternatingRowStyle	Defines the style properties for every alternate row in the DetailsView.
EditRowStyle	Defines the style properties for the row in EditView (When you click Edit button for a row, the row will appear in this style).
RowStyle	Defines the style properties of the rows of the DetailsView.
PagerStyle	Defines the style properties of Pager of the DetailsView. (If AllowPaging=true, the page number row appears in this style)
EmptyDataRowStyle	Defines the style properties of the empty row, which appears if there is no records in the data source.
HeaderStyle	Defines the style properties of the header of the DetailsView. (The column header appears in this style.)
FooterStyle	Defines the style properties of the footer of DetailsView.

Table 4-7 : Style Properties for DetailsView control

Appearance Properties of the DetailsView Control	
CellPadding	Indicates the amount of space in pixel between the cells and the border of the DetailsView.
CellSpacing	Indicates the amount of space in pixel between cells.
GridLines	Both/Horizontal/Vertical/None. Indicates whether GrdiLines should appear or not. if yes Horizontal, Vertical or Both.
HorizontalAlign	Indicates the horizontal alignment of the DetailsView.
EmptyDataText	Indicates the text to appear when there is no record in the data source.
BackImageUrl	Indicates the location of the image that should display as a background of the DetailsView.
Caption	Gets or sets the caption of the DetailsView.
CaptionAlign	left/center/right. Gets or sets the horizontal position of the DetailsView caption.

Table 4-8 : Apperance Properties for DetailsView control

State Properties of DetailsView Control	
Rows	Gets the collection of objects that represent the rows in the DetailsView.
FooterRow	Returns a DetailsViewRow object that represents the footer of the DetailsView.
HeaderRow	Returns a DetailsViewRow object that represents the header of the DetailsView.
PageCount	Gets the number of the pages required to display the records of the data source.
PageIndex	Gets or sets the 0-based page index.
DataKeyNames	Gets an array that contains the names of the primary key field of the currently displayed rows in the DetailsViewRow.
DataKeys	Gets a collection of DataKey objects that represent the value of the primary key fields set in DataKeyNames property of the DetailsViewRow.

Table 4-9 : State Properties for DetailsView control

Events of the DetailsView Control	
ItemCommand	Fires when any clickable element on the control is clicked.
ItemCreated	Fires after DetailsView fully creates all rows of the record.
ItemDeleting, ItemDeleted	Both event fires when current record is deleted. The first one fires before and other fires after record is deleted.
ItemInserting, ItemInserted	Both event fires when an item is inserted. The first one fires before and second after the item is created.
ItemUpdating, ItemUpdated	Both event fires when an item is updated. The first one fires before and second fires after the record is updated.
ModeChanging, ModeChanged	Both event fires when DetailsView change its display mode. The first one fires before and second fires after display mode is changed.
PageIndexChanging, PageIndexChanged	Both event fires when the DetailsView move to another record. The first one fires before and second fires after page is changed.

Table 4-10 :Events for DetailsView control

Example of DetailsView Control

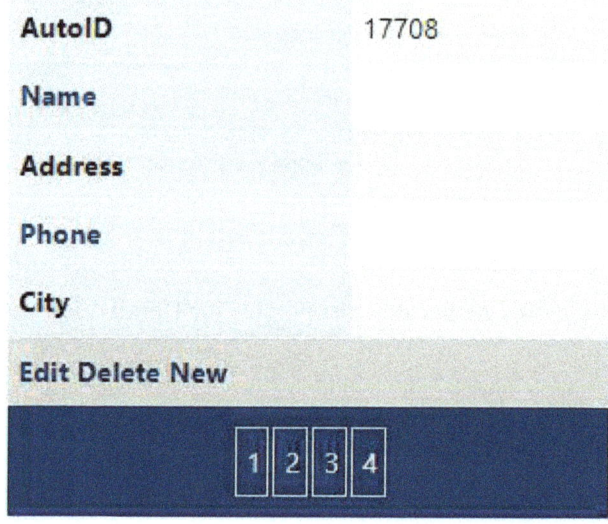

Source Code

```
// DetailsView control
<asp:DetailsView ID="DetailsView1" runat="Server" CellPadding="4" ForeColor="#333333"
    GridLines="None"
     Width="100%" DataSourceID="SqlDataSource1" AllowPaging="True" AutoGenerateRows
         ="False" DataKeyNames="AutoID"
     AutoGenerateDeleteButton="True" AutoGenerateEditButton="True"
         AutoGenerateInsertButton="True" >
        <FooterStyle BackColor="#5D7B9D" Font-Bold="True" ForeColor="White" />
        <CommandRowStyle BackColor="#E2DED6" Font-Bold="True" />
        <EditRowStyle BackColor="#999999" />
        <RowStyle BackColor="#F7F6F3" ForeColor="#333333" />
        <PagerStyle BackColor="#284775" ForeColor="White" HorizontalAlign="Center" />
        <FieldHeaderStyle BackColor="#E9ECF1" Font-Bold="True" />
        <HeaderStyle BackColor="#5D7B9D" Font-Bold="True" ForeColor="White" />
        <AlternatingRowStyle BackColor="White" ForeColor="#284775" />
        <Fields>
            <asp:TemplateField HeaderText="AutoID">
                <ItemTemplate>
                    <%# Eval("AutoID") %>
                </ItemTemplate>
            </asp:TemplateField>
            <asp:BoundField DataField="Name" HeaderText="Name" />
            <asp:BoundField DataField="Address" HeaderText="Address" />
            <asp:BoundField DataField="Phone" HeaderText="Phone" />
            <asp:BoundField DataField="City" HeaderText="City" />
        </Fields>
    </asp:DetailsView>
```

```
// SqlDataSource control
    <asp:SqlDataSource ID="SqlDataSource1" runat="server" ConnectionStr
        ConnectionStrings:ConnStr %>'
     SelectCommand="Select * FROM SampleForTutorials ORDER BY [Name]"
     DeleteCommand="Delete FROM SampleForTutorials WHERE AutoID = @AutoI
     UpdateCommand="UPDATE SampleForTutorials SET Name = @Name, Address
         @Phone, City = @City WHERE AutoID = @AutoID"
     InsertCommand="INSERT INTO SampleForTutorials (Name, Address, Phone
         (@Name, @Address, @Phone, @City)">
        <DeleteParameters>
            <asp:Parameter Name="AutoID" />
        </DeleteParameters>
        <UpdateParameters>
            <asp:Parameter Name="AutoID" Type="Int32" />
            <asp:Parameter Name="Name" Type="string" Size="50" />
            <asp:Parameter Name="Address" Type="string" Size="200" />
            <asp:Parameter Name="Phone"  Type="string" Size="50" />
            <asp:Parameter Name="City" Type="string" Size="20" />
        </UpdateParameters>
        <InsertParameters>
            <asp:Parameter Name="Name" Type="string" Size="50" />
            <asp:Parameter Name="Address" Type="string" Size="200" />
            <asp:Parameter Name="Phone" Type="string" Size="50" />
            <asp:Parameter Name="City" Type="string" Size="20" />
            <asp:Parameter Name="AutoID" Type="Int32" />
        </InsertParameters>
    </asp:SqlDataSource>
```

• • •

4.5 FormView Control

FormView is a new data-bound control that is nothing but a templated version of DetailsView control. The major difference between DetailsView and FormView is, here user need to define the rendering template for each item.

Its properties like BackColor, ForeColor, BorderColor, BorderStyle, BorderWidth, Height etc. are implemented through style properites of <tahle> tag.

Following are some important properties that are very useful.

Templates of the FormView Control	
EditItemTemplate	The template that is used when a record is being edited.
InsertItemTemplate	The template that is used when a record is being created.
ItemTemplate	The template that is used to render the record to display only.

Table 4-11 : Templates for FormView control

Methods of the FormView Control	
ChangeMode	ReadOnly/Insert/Edit. Change the working mode of the control from the current to the defined FormViewMode type.
InsertItem	Used to insert the record into database. This method must be called when the DetailsView control is in insert mode.
UpdateItem	Used to update the current record into database. This method must be called when DetailsView control is in edit mode.
DeleteItem	Used to delete the current record from database.

Table 4-12 : Methods for FormView control

Example of FormView Control

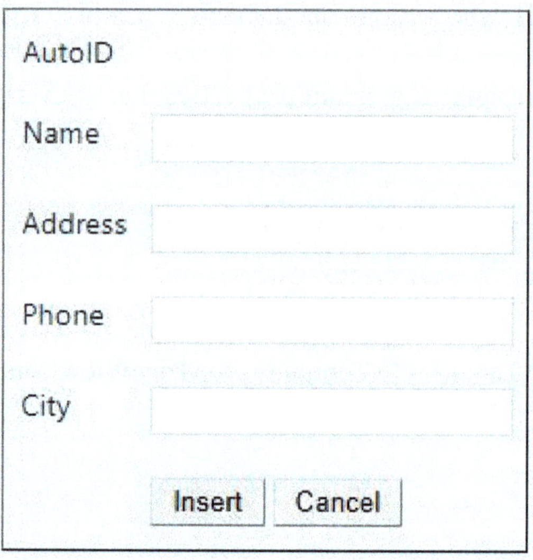

Source Code

```
// FormView control ////////////////////////////////
<asp:FormView ID="FormView1" runat="server" CellPadding="4" ForeColor="#333333"
    DataKeyNames="AutoID" DataSourceID="SqlDataSource1" AllowPaging="true">
        <FooterStyle BackColor="#507CD1" Font-Bold="True" ForeColor="White" />
        <RowStyle BackColor="#EFF3FB" />
        <PagerStyle BackColor="#2461BF" ForeColor="White" HorizontalAlign="Center" />
        <HeaderStyle BackColor="#507CD1" Font-Bold="True" ForeColor="White" />
        <ItemTemplate>
            <table border="1">
                <tr>
                    <td>AutoID</td>
                    <td><%# Eval("AutoID") %></td>
                </tr>
                <tr>
                    <td>Name</td>
                    <td><%# Eval("Name") %></td>
                </tr>
                <tr>
                    <td>Address</td>
                    <td><%# Eval("Address") %></td>
                </tr>
                <tr>
                    <td>Phone</td>
                    <td><%# Eval("Phone") %></td>
                </tr>
```

```
            <tr>
                <td>City</td>
                <td><%# Eval("City") %></td>
            </tr>
            <tr>
                <td> </td>
                <td>
                    <asp:Button ID="btnEdit" runat="Server" CommandName="Edit" Text
                        ="Edit" />
                    <asp:Button ID="btnInsert" runat="Server" CommandName="New"
                        Text="New" />
                    <asp:Button ID="btnDelete" runat="Server" CommandName="Delete"
                        Text="Delete" OnClientClick="return confirm('Are you sure
                        to Delete?');" />
                </td>
            </tr>
        </table>
    </ItemTemplate>
```

```
<EditItemTemplate>
    <table border="1">
        <tr>
            <td>AutoID</td>
            <td><%# Eval("AutoID") %></td>
        </tr>
        <tr>
            <td>Name</td>
            <td><asp:TextBox ID="TextBox1" runat="Server" Text='<%# Bind("Name"
                )%>'></asp:TextBox></td>
        </tr>
        <tr>
            <td>Address</td>
            <td><asp:TextBox ID="TextBox2" runat="Server" Text='<%# Bind
                ("Address")%>'></asp:TextBox></td>
        </tr>
        <tr>
            <td>Phone</td>
            <td><asp:TextBox ID="TextBox3" runat="Server" Text='<%# Bind("Phone"
                )%>'></asp:TextBox></td>
        </tr>
        <tr>
            <td>City</td>
            <td><asp:TextBox ID="TextBox4" runat="Server" Text='<%# Bind("City"
                )%>'></asp:TextBox></td>
        </tr>
```

```
    <tr>
        <td> </td>
        <td>
            <asp:Button ID="btnUpdate" runat="Server" CommandName="Update"
                Text="Update" />
            <asp:Button ID="Button1" runat="Server" CommandName="Cancel"
                Text="Cancel" />
        </td>
    </tr>
  </table>
</EditItemTemplate>
<InsertItemTemplate>
    <table border="1">
        <tr>
            <td>AutoID</td>
            <td><%# Eval("AutoID") %></td>
        </tr>
        <tr>
            <td>Name</td>
            <td><asp:TextBox ID="TextBox1" runat="Server" Text='<%# Bind("Name"
                )%>'></asp:TextBox></td>
        </tr>
        <tr>
            <td>Address</td>
            <td><asp:TextBox ID="TextBox2" runat="Server" Text='<%# Bind
                ("Address")%>'></asp:TextBox></td>
        </tr>
```

```
            <tr>
                <td>Phone</td>
                <td><asp:TextBox ID="TextBox3" runat="Server" Text='<%# Bind("Phone"
                    )%>'></asp:TextBox></td>
            </tr>
            <tr>
                <td>City</td>
                <td><asp:TextBox ID="TextBox4" runat="Server" Text='<%# Bind("City"
                    )%>'></asp:TextBox></td>
            </tr>
            <tr>
                <td> </td>
                <td>
                    <asp:Button ID="btnSave" runat="Server" CommandName="insert"
                        Text="Insert" />
                    <asp:Button ID="Button1" runat="Server" CommandName="Cancel"
                        Text="Cancel" />
                </td>
            </tr>
        </table>
    </InsertItemTemplate>
</asp:FormView>
```

```
// SqlDataSource Control ///////////////////////////////////
<asp:SqlDataSource ID="SqlDataSource1" runat="server" ConnectionString='<%$
    ConnectionStrings:ConnStr %>'
 SelectCommand="Select * FROM SampleForTutorials ORDER BY [Name]"
 DeleteCommand="Delete FROM SampleForTutorials WHERE AutoID = @AutoID"
 UpdateCommand="UPDATE SampleForTutorials SET Name = @Name, Address = @Address, Phone =
     @Phone, City = @City WHERE AutoID = @AutoID"
 InsertCommand="INSERT INTO SampleForTutorials (Name, Address, Phone, City) VALUES
     (@Name, @Address, @Phone, @City)">
    <DeleteParameters>
        <asp:Parameter Name="AutoID" />
    </DeleteParameters>
    <UpdateParameters>
        <asp:Parameter Name="AutoID" Type="Int32" />
        <asp:Parameter Name="Name" Type="string" Size="50" />
        <asp:Parameter Name="Address" Type="string" Size="200" />
        <asp:Parameter Name="Phone"  Type="string" Size="50" />
        <asp:Parameter Name="City" Type="string" Size="20" />
    </UpdateParameters>
    <InsertParameters>
        <asp:Parameter Name="Name" Type="string" Size="50" />
        <asp:Parameter Name="Address" Type="string" Size="200" />
        <asp:Parameter Name="Phone" Type="string" Size="50" />
        <asp:Parameter Name="City" Type="string" Size="20" />
        <asp:Parameter Name="AutoID" Type="Int32" />
    </InsertParameters>
</asp:SqlDataSource>
```

CHAPTER V

Advanced ASP.NET

5.1 ASP AJAX

AJAX is about updating parts of a web page, without reloading the whole page.

What is AJAX?

- AJAX = Asynchronous JavaScript and XML.
- AJAX is a technique for creating fast and dynamic web pages.
- AJAX allows web pages to be updated asynchronously by exchanging small amounts of data with the server behind the scenes. This means that it is possible to update parts of a web page, without reloading the whole page.
- Classic web pages, (which do not use AJAX) must reload the entire page if the content should change.
- Examples of applications using AJAX: Google Maps, Gmail, Youtube, and Facebook tabs.

How AJAX Works

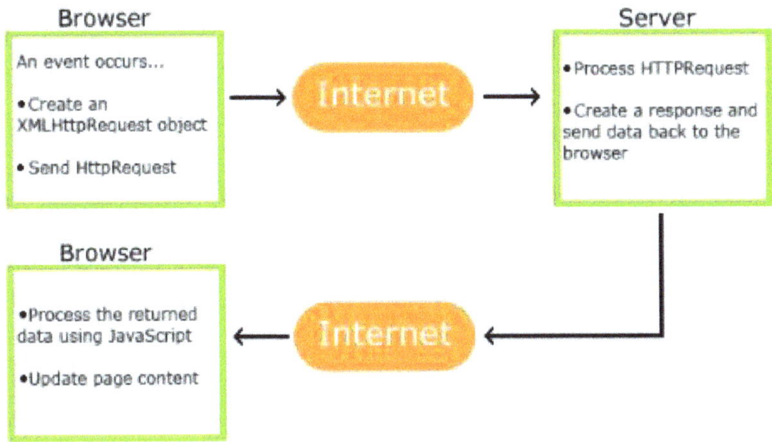

Figure 5-1 : Ajax WorkFlow

AJAX is Based on Internet Standards

AJAX is based on internet standards, and uses a combination of:

- XMLHttpRequest object (to exchange data asynchronously with a server)
- JavaScript/DOM (to display/interact with the information)
- CSS (to style the data)
- XML (often used as the format for transferring data)

Advantages

- Reduces the traffic travels between the client and the server.
- No cross browser pain.
- Better interactivity and responsiveness.
- With AJAX, several multi purpose applications and features can be handled using a single web page(SPA).
- API's are good because those work with HTTP method and JavaScrtipt.

Disadvantages

- Search engines like Google would not be able to index an AJAX application.
- It is totally built-in JavaScript code. If any user disables JS in the browser, it won't work.
- The server information can not be accessed within AJAX.
- Security is less in AJAX applications as all the files are downloaded at client side.
- The data of all requests is URL-encoded, which increases the size of the request.

AJAX ASP Example

The following example will demonstrate how a web page can communicate with a web server while a user type characters in an input field:

Start typing a name in the input field below:

First name:

Suggestions:

Example Explained

In the example above, when a user types a character in the input field, a function called "showHint()" is executed.

The function is triggered by the onkeyup event.

Here is the HTML code:

```
<html>
<head>
<script>
function showHint(str) {
    if (str.length == 0) {
        document.getElementById("txtHint").innerHTML = "";
        return;
    } else {
        var xmlhttp = new XMLHttpRequest();
        xmlhttp.onreadystatechange = function() {
            if (this.readyState == 4 && this.status == 200) {
                document.getElementById("txtHint").innerHTML = this.responseText;
            }
        };
        xmlhttp.open("GET", "gethint.asp?q=" + str, true);
        xmlhttp.send();
    }
}
</script>
</head>
<body>

<p><b>Start typing a name in the input field below:</b></p>
<form>
First name: <input type="text" onkeyup="showHint(this.value)">
</form>
<p>Suggestions: <span id="txtHint"></span></p>
</body>
</html>
```

Code explanation:

First, check if the input field is empty (str.length == 0). If it is, clear the content of the txtHint placeholder and exit the function.

However, if the input field is not empty, do the following:

- Create an XMLHttpRequest object
- Create the function to be executed when the server response is ready
- Send the request off to an ASP file (gethint.asp) on the server
- Notice that q parameter is added gethint.asp?q="+str
- The str variable holds the content of the input field

• • •

5.2 Working with XML

Introduction of XML

XML stands for Extensible markup language. XML is a cross-platform, hardware and software independent, text based markup language, which enables you to store data in a structured format by using meaningful tags. XML stores structured data in XML documents that are similar to databases. Notice that unlike Databases, XML documents store data in the form of plain text, which can be used across platforms.

The following code defines the structure of an XML document that will store data related to books:

```
<?xml version="1.0"?>
<Books>
  <Book bid="B001">
    <Title> Understanding XML </Title>
    <Price> $30 </Price>
    <author>
      <FirstName> Lily </FirstName>
      <LastName>
        Hicks <LastName>
        </author>
  </Book>
  <Book bid="B002">
    <Title> .NET Framework </Title>
    <Price> $45 </Price>
    <author>
      <FirstName> Jasmine </FirstName>
      <LastName>
        Williams <LastName>
        </author>
  </Book>
</Books>
```

.NET Support for XML

The .NET Framework has extensive support for working with XML documents. IN the .NET framework, the support for XML documents includes:

1. XML namespace
2. XML designer
3. XML Web Server control
4. XML Document Object Model Support

1. XML namespace

The System.Xml namespace provides a rich set of classes for processing XML data. The commonly used classes for working with XML data are:

- **XmlTextReader:** Provides forward only access to a stream of XML data and checks whether or not an XML document is well formed. This class neither creates as in-memory structure nor validates the XML document against the DTD. You can declare an object of the XmlTextReader class by including the System.Xml namespace in the application. The syntax to declare an object of this class is as follows:

  ```
  XmlTextReader reader = new XmlTextReader("XML1.xml");
  ```

  It is important to note that the .xml file you pass as an argument to the constructor of the XmlTextReader class exists in the \WINNT\System32 folder.

- **XmlTextWriter:** Provides forward only way of generating streams or files containing XML data that conforms to W3C XML 1.0. If you want to declare an object of the XmlTextWriter class, you must include the System.Xml. The syntax to decare an object of this class is as follows:

  ```
  XmlTextWriter writer = new XmlTextWriter(Response.Output);
  ```

  Here Response.Output represents an outgoing HTTP response stream to which you want to send the XML data.

- **XmlDocument:** Provides navigating and edinting features of the nodes in an XML document tree. XmlDocument is the most frequently used class in ASP.NET applications that use XML documents. It also supports W3C XML DOM. XML DOM is an in-memory representation of an XML document. It represents data in the form of hierarchically organized object nodes and allows you to programmatically access and manipulate the elements and attributes present in an XML document.

  XmlDocument doc = new XmlDocument();

- **XmlDataDocument:** Provides support for XML and relational data in W3C XML DOM. You can use this class with a dataset to provide relational and non-relational views of the same set of data. This class is primarily used when you want to access the functions of ADO.NET. The syntax to declare an object of this class is as follows:

  DataSet ds=new DataSet();
XmlDataDocument doc=new XmlDocument(ds);

There are a number of reasons to use XmlDataDocument:

It gives you the freedom to work with any data by using the DOM.

There is synchronization between an XmlDatadocument and a DataSet, and any changes in one will be reflected in the other.

When an XML document is loaded into an XmlDatadocument, the schema is preserved.

You need to include System.Xml namespace.

- **XmlPathDocument:** Provides a read-only cache for XML document processing by using XSLT. This class is optimizied for XSLT processing and does not check for the conformity of W3C DOM. For this reason, you can create an instance of this class to process an XML document faster. To create an instance of the XPathDocument class, you need to include the System.Xml.XPath namespace in the application. The Syntax to declare an object of this class is as follows:

  XmlPathDocument doc=new XmlPathDocument("XML1.xml");

- **XmlNodeReader:** Provides forward-only access to the data represented by the XmlDocument or XmlDataDocument class. If you want to create an instance of the XmlNodeReader class, you need to include the System.Xml namespace. The syntax to declare an object of this class is as follows:

```
XmlDocument doc=new XmlPathDocument();
XmlNodeReader reader=new XmlNodeReader(doc);
```

- **XslTransform:** Provides support for a XSLT 1.0 style sheet syntax that enables you to transform an XML document by using XSL style sheets. If you want to create an instance of the XslTransform class, you need to include the System.Xml.Xsl namespace in the application. The syntax to declare an object of this class is as follows:

```
Xsltransform xslt = new XslTransform ();
```

2. XML Designer

Visual Studio .NET provides the XML designer that you can use to create and edit XML documents. For example, if you need to create an XML document that contains the details of books available in an online bookstore, you need to perform the following steps by using the XML designer of Visual Studio .NET:

1. Create a new ASP.NET Web application.
2. Select the Add New Item option
3. Select XML File as the template from the right pane. Specify the name as "books.xml" and click open.
4. The XML designer is displayed. The XML designer has automatically generated a line that notifies the browser that the document being processed is an XML document, as displayed in the figure:

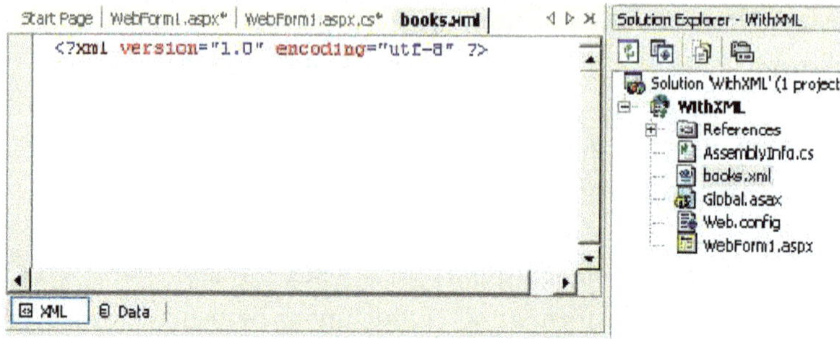

5. At the bottom of the designer window, there are two tabs, XML and Data. In the XML tab enter the following lines of code after the first line in the XML designer:

```
<?xml version="1.0" encoding="utf-8" ?>
<books>
    <book>
        <bookid> B001 </bookid>
        <title> Understanding XML </title>
        <Price> $30 </Price>
        <Author>
            <FirstName> Lily </FirstName>
            <LastName> Hicks </LastName>
        </Author>
    </book>
    <book>
        <bookid> B002 </bookid>
        <title> .NET Framework </title>
        <Price> $45 </Price>
        <Author>
            <FirstName> Jasmine </FirstName>
            <LastName> Williams </LastName>
        </Author>
    </book>
</books>
```

The Data view displays the XML data represented by the XML document. When you switch to the Data view, the data appears, as displayed in the following figure:

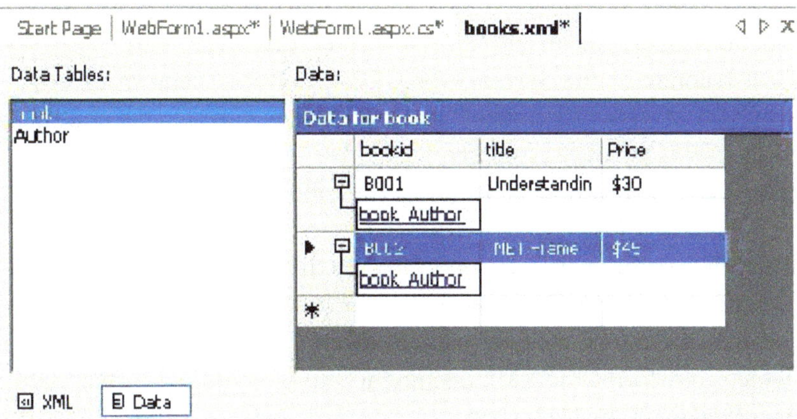

In addition to just viewing data in the Data view, you can also add data directly to an existing XML document. For this, just click on the new row below the existing data and enter your values, and shown in the figure:

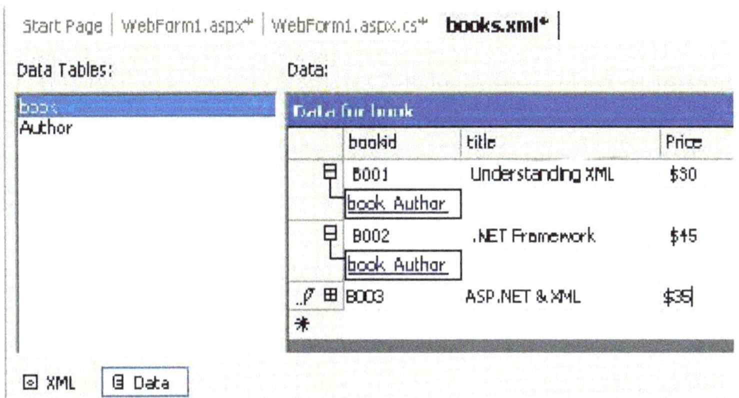

3. XML Web Server Control

An XML Web Server control is used to display the contents of an XML document without formatting or using XSL Transformations. You can optionally specify a XSLT style sheet that formats the XML document before it is displayed in an XML server control. The XML Web Server control belongs to the System.Web.UI.WebControls namespace. You can add an XML Web Server control to a Web form by dragging the control from the Web forms tab of the toolbox.

The XML Web Server control has the following properties:

1. **DocumentSource:** Allows you to specify the URL or the path of the XML document to be displayed in the Web form.
2. **TransformSource:** Allows you to specify the URL of the XSLT file, which transforms the XML document into the required format before it is displayed in the Web form.
3. **Document:** Allows you to specify a reference to an object of the XMLDocument class. This property is available only at runtime.
4. **Transform:** Allows you to specify a reference to an object of the XMLTransform class. This property is available only at runtime.

4.XML Document Object Model Support

When you want to access and display XML data in Web Applications, you use the XML Web server control and set its properties at design time. In certain situation, you may need to display the XML data based on specific conditions. In such cases, you will have to access the XML data programmatically.

An XML document consists of elements and attributes. For this reason, you can access XML data programmatically. Note that XML DOM allows you to access and manipulate the elements and attributes present in an XML document programmatically.

To implement XML DOM, the .NET framework provides a set of additional classes included in the System.Xml namespace. These classes enable you to access the XML data programmatically. Some of the classes in the System.Xml namespace are as follows:

- **XmlDocumentType:** Represents the DTD used by an XML document.
- **XmlElement:** Represents one element from an XML document.
- **XmlAttribute:** Represents one attribute of an element.

Bind XML Data to Web Form Controls

An XML document cannot be directly bound to server controls. To implement data binding, you first need to load the XML document into a DataSet. Then, you can bind server control with this DataSet.

The Dataset object has a ReadXml method, which is used to read data into the DataSet from an XML file. The ReadXml method can read XML documents from the Stream, File, TextReader, and XmlReader sources. The synatx for the ReadXml method is as follows:

The XmlReadMode parameter can take any of the values listed in the following table:

VALUES	DESCIPTION
Auto	Checks the XML document and selects the action accordingly from the following choices: 1. If the DataSet already has schema or the document contains an inline schema, it sets XmlReadMode to ReadSchema. 2. If the DataSet does not already have a schema and the document does not contain an inline schema, it sets XmlReadMode to InferSchema
DiffGram	Reads a Diffgram, which is a format that contains both the original and the current values of the data, and applies changes from the DiffGram to the DataSet.
Fragment	The default namespace is read as the inline schema
IgnoreSchema	Ignores any inline schema and reads data into the existing DataSet schema.
InferSchema	Ignores any inline schema and instead infers schema from the data and loads the data.
ReadSchema	Reads any inline schema and loads the data. If the DataSet already has a schema, new tables may be added to the schema but an exception is thrown if any tables in the inline schema already exist in the DataSet.

Table 5-1: XmlReadMode Parameter

• • •

5.3 LINQ

LINQ(Language Integrated Query) introduced in VS 2008. Even though you don't know query languages(SQL,XML,...) you can write queries by using LINQ (In C# and VB.NET). Because you write queries by using language keywords and familiar words.

We can write the LINQ queries for the following :

- Collection of Objects (should support IEnumerable or generic IEnumerable)
- XML
- ADO.NET

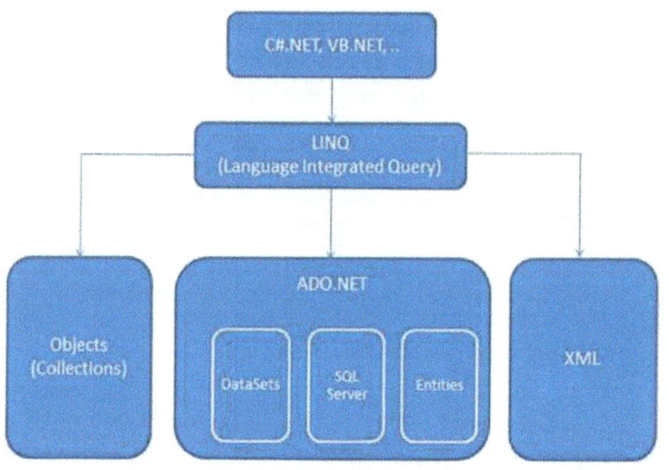

Figure 5-3 : LINQ Structure

Example:

Book. cs

```
public class Books
{
    public string ID {get; set;}
    public string Title { get; set; }
    public decimal Price { get; set; }
    public DateTime DateOfRelease { get; set; }

    public static List<Books> GetBooks()
    {
        List<Books> list = new List<Books>();
        list.Add(new Books { ID = "001",
          Title = "Programming in C#",
          Price = 634.76m,
          DateOfRelease = Convert.ToDateTime("2010-02-05") });

        list.Add(new Books { ID = "002",
          Title = "Learn Java in 30 days",
          Price = 250.76m,
          DateOfRelease = Convert.ToDateTime("2011-08-15") });

        list.Add(new Books { ID = "003",
          Title = "Programming in ASP.Net 4.0",
          Price = 700.00m,
          DateOfRelease = Convert.ToDateTime("2011-02-05") });

        list.Add(new Books { ID = "004",
          Title = "VB.Net Made Easy",
          Price = 500.99m,
          DateOfRelease = Convert.ToDateTime("2011-12-31") });

        list.Add(new Books { ID = "005",
          Title = "Programming in C",
          Price = 314.76m,
          DateOfRelease = Convert.ToDateTime("2010-02-05") });

        list.Add(new Books { ID = "006",
          Title = "Programming in C++",
          Price = 456.76m,
          DateOfRelease = Convert.ToDateTime("2010-02-05") });

        list.Add(new Books { ID = "007",
          Title = "Datebase Developement",
          Price = 1000.76m,
          DateOfRelease = Convert.ToDateTime("2010-02-05") });


        return list;
    }
```

The web page using this class has a simple label control, which displays the titles of the books. The Page_Load event creates a list of books and returns the titles by using LINQ query:

```
public partial class simplequery : System.Web.UI.Page
{
    protected void Page_Load(object sender, EventArgs e)
    {
        List<Books> books = Books.GetBooks();
        var booktitles = from b in books select b.Title;

        foreach (var title in booktitles)
            lblbooks.Text += String.Format("{0} <br />", title);
    }
}
```

When the page is executed, the label displays the results of the query:

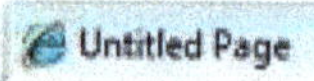

Programming in C#
Learn Jave in 30 days
Programming in ASP.Net 4.0
VB.Net Made Easy
Programming in C
Programming in C++
Datebase Developement

The above LINQ expression:
var booktitles = from b in books
select b.Title;
Is equivalent to the following SQL query:
SELECT Title from Books

• • •

5.4 Stored Procedure

What is Stored Procedure?

In DBMS (database management system), a stored procedure is a set of Structured Query Language i.e. (SQL). They are stored in database server (SQL Server). Stored procedure is a group of T-SQL statements which performs one or more specific task in a single execution plan. We can create group of Transact-SQL statements and Store in SP.

There are 3 different types of SP's (System SP's, User Defined SP's and Extended SP's).

- **Note :** In DBMS Stored Procedure is denoted by SP.
- **System SP's :** It is stored in master database (pre-fixed "sp_" and usually perform the task for sql server functions.
- **User Defined SP's :** These custom SP's are created by user for implementing certain task in their applications (like INSERT, UPDATE, DELETE and SELECT).
- **Extended SP's :** Depreciated (No longer in USE).

Types of Parameters available in Stored Procedures

- **Input Parameter :** We can pass any number of input parameters to SP function.
- **Output Parameter :** We can output any number of output parameters from SP function.
- **Return Parameter :** But we can return only one/single return parameter from SP function.

Advantages of using Stored Procedures in ASP.NET

1. Stored procedures are special objects available in database server and they are very fast when compared to ordinary t-sql statements and thus helps to improve performance both sql and application.
2. Stored Procedures offers great performance since they are pre-compiled code for other subsequent calls and they are not pre-compiled code for first time but for other subsequent call they are pre-compiled because when we execute SP for first time in database server, database server makes an entry of SP in its cache memory once an entry is made in cache memory for other subsequent call it will call that SP directly from the cache memory. Hence stored procedures are pre-compiled for other subsequent calls. If input value changes or output value changes SP will

remain in cache memory with the same entry. If you are looking out to execute a group of sql query without compromising the memory then SP will provide a great performance. It is a best practice to use SP's in the DOT.NET projects.

3. Since SP are located at database server we can call that SP for any of asp.net c# pages for any number of time.
4. Stored procedures are faster as compared to normal T-SQL statements.
5. In a single SP execution plan we can execute a bunch of SQL statements.
6. Stored procedures are easy to maintain. If any changes occurs just we need to update single stored procedure located at database server, single update will reflect in all pages. Instead of going and changing all queries in all the pages just we need to update a single SP file.
7. We can reuse the SP code again and again means we can call SP function again and again without compromising the performance and memory.
8. It provides query encapsulation and offer simple sp function. So it means sp provide better security to your data queries.
9. SP enhances the security controls means users can be granted permission to execute a stored procedure which makes better security to data.
10. It trims down network traffic by executing a single line of function name over the network instead of executing hundred lines of T-SQL statements.

Implementing Stored Procedures in ASP.NET

In order to implement sp in asp.net project first we need to create a sp in database server or sql server. So let's open up Microsoft SQL Server 2008 and select a database (if you have not created a database then create a new one). Now maximize the database folder and also maximize the "programmability" folder inside the "programmability" you will find stored procedure folder.

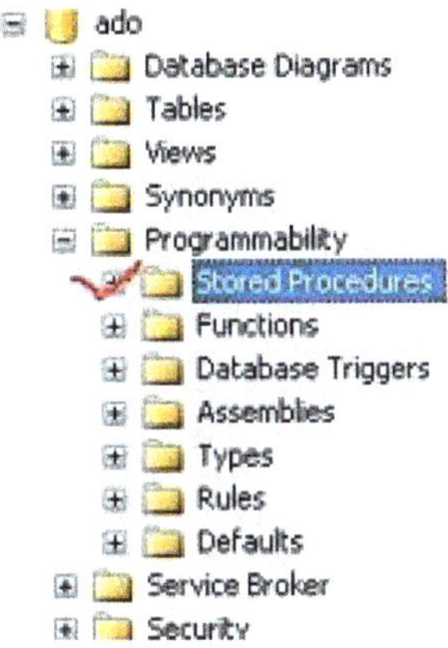

Sample Code SP:

Example: Step by Step Insert data using stored procedure in asp.net c#

Step 1: Create a Simple Screen on ASP.NET Page

First step create a simple input screen to insert the data into database in asp.net page. Here in this example created the input put form in default.aspx page.

Insert records using stored procedure

Property Name	
Property Address	
Property Price	
Available units (1 BHK)	
HiddenField - txtPropertyID	
Update Property	Add Property

```
<table border="1" cellpadding="5" style="border-collapse:collapse;
font-family:Verdana; font-size:12px;">


        <tr>
        <td>Property Name</td>
        <td><asp:TextBox ID="txtpropertyname" runat="server"></asp:TextBox></td>
        </tr>
        <tr>
        <td>Property Address</td>
        <td><asp:TextBox ID="txtpropertyaddress" runat="server">
</asp:TextBox></td>
        </tr>
        <tr>

        <td>Property Price</td>
        <td><asp:TextBox ID="txtpropertyprice" runat="server"></asp:TextBox></td>
        </tr>

        <tr>
        <td>Available units (1 BHK) </td>
        <td><asp:TextBox ID="txtavailableunits" runat="server">
</asp:TextBox></td>
        </tr>

        <tr>
        <td colspan="2">
         <asp:HiddenField ID="txtPropertyID" runat="server" />
        </td>

        </tr>
        <tr>
        <td colspan="2">



                <asp:Button ID="btn_Update" runat="server" Text="Update P
                    onclick="btn_Update_Click" />

                     

                    <asp:Button ID="btn_Insert" runat="server" Text="Add
                    onclick="btn_Insert_Click" />


        </td>
        </tr>
        <tr>

        <td>Output : </td>
           <td>   <asp:Label ID="lbloutput" runat="server" Text="">
</asp:Label></td>
        </tr>
        </table>
```

Step 2: Create a SQL Table For Above Screen

In this step we have to create a sql table for above input screen.

```
CREATE TABLE [dbo].[propertylisting](
    [property_id] [int] IDENTITY(1,1) NOT NULL,
    [propertyname] [varchar](150) NULL,
    [propertyaddress] [varchar](500) NULL,
    [propertyprice] [money] NULL,
    [availableunits] [varchar](50) NULL,
 CONSTRAINT [PK_propertylisting] PRIMARY KEY CLUSTERED
(
    [property_id] ASC
)WITH (PAD_INDEX  = OFF, STATISTICS_NORECOMPUTE  = OFF, IGNORE_DUP_KEY = OFF,
ALLOW_ROW_LOCKS  = ON, ALLOW_PAGE_LOCKS  = ON) ON [PRIMARY]
) ON [PRIMARY]
```

Step 3: Create a Stored Procedure with Input Parameter, Output Parameter and Return Parameter

This is the main step of this example because here where we will create a stored procedure with input parameters to accept the values from the asp.net screen and output parameter which will be output with last inserted record ID.

```
USE [property]
GO
/****** Object:  StoredProcedure [dbo].[usp_insertpropertylisting]    Script Date:
06/29/2014 18:05:03 ******/
SET ANSI_NULLS ON
GO
SET QUOTED_IDENTIFIER ON
GO
CREATE  PROCEDURE [dbo].[usp_insertpropertylisting]
    @propertyname varchar(150),
    @propertyaddress varchar(500),
    @propertyprice money,
    @availableunits varchar(100),
    @propertyID int output
AS
BEGIN

    INSERT into propertylisting(propertyname,propertyaddress,
    propertyprice,availableunits)

    VALUES

    (@propertyname,@propertyaddress, @propertyprice,@availableunits)

    SET @propertyID = SCOPE_IDENTITY()

    RETURN @propertyID
END
```

Step 4: Call Stored Procedure in ASP.NET C# Code

Now let's call the stored procedure in default.aspx page.In order to call stored procedure in asp.net page, first we need to create a sql connection and import the "using System.Data.SqlClient;" namespace.

SQL Connection

```
<connectionStrings>
  <add name="Conn" connectionString="Data Source=guru\\sqlexpress;Initial
Catalog=property;Integrated Security=True"/>
</connectionStrings>
```

SQL Namespace

```
using System.Configuration;
using System.Data;
using System.Data.SqlClient;
```

In our input from which we have created in default.aspx page there we have a submit button. Now inside submit button click we will call our stored procedure code.

```
protected void btn_Insert_Click(object sender, EventArgs e)
{
    string conn = "";
    conn = ConfigurationManager.ConnectionStrings["Conn"].ToString();
    SqlConnection objsqlconn = new SqlConnection(conn);
    try
    {
        if (txtpropertyname.Text != "")
        {

            objsqlconn.Open();
            SqlCommand objcmd = new SqlCommand("usp_insertpropertylisting",
objsqlconn);
            objcmd.CommandType = CommandType.StoredProcedure;

            SqlParameter property_id = objcmd.Parameters.Add("@propertyID",
SqlDbType.Int);

            property_id.Direction = ParameterDirection.Output;


            SqlParameter property_name = objcmd.Parameters.Add("@propertyname",
SqlDbType.VarChar);
            property_name.Value = txtpropertyname.Text;

            SqlParameter property_addr = objcmd.Parameters.Add("@propertyaddress",
SqlDbType.VarChar);
            property_addr.Value = txtpropertyaddress.Text;


            SqlParameter property_price = objcmd.Parameters.Add("@propertyprice",
SqlDbType.Money);
            property_price.Value = txtpropertyprice.Text;

            SqlParameter available_units = objcmd.Parameters.Add("@availableunits",
SqlDbType.VarChar);
            available_units.Value = txtavailableunits.Text;

            objcmd.ExecuteNonQuery();

            ClearAll();
            //Response.Redirect("Default.aspx");

            lbloutput.Text = "Record inserted successfully. ID = " +
 property_id.Value.ToString();
        }




        }
        catch (Exception ex)
        {
            Response.Write(ex.Message.ToString());
        }
        finally
        {
            objsqlconn.Close();
        }

    }
```

Display Data using stored procedure in ASP.NET

Step 1: Write Stored Procedure

```
USE [property]
GO
/****** Object:  StoredProcedure [dbo].[usp_loadproperties]    Script Date:
07/01/2014 00:03:42 ******/
SET ANSI_NULLS ON
GO
SET QUOTED_IDENTIFIER ON
GO
CREATE PROCEDURE [dbo].[usp_loadproperties]
    @PropertyID int
AS
BEGIN


    if(@PropertyID != 0)
    begin
    SELECT * from propertylisting where property_id=@PropertyID
    end
    else
    begin
    SELECT * from propertylisting
    end

END
```

Step 2: Displaying Records in ASP.NET Page

To display records in aspx page we will use gridview tool from toolbox. So let's add a gridview tool to aspx page.

```
<asp:GridView ID="grdloadproperties" runat="server"></asp:GridView>
```

Step 3: Call the Stored Procedure

In the default.aspx page load event we will load the gridbox as shown in below code snippet.

```
protected void Page_Load(object sender, EventArgs e)
{
       string conn = "";
       conn = ConfigurationManager.ConnectionStrings["Conn"].ToString();
       SqlConnection objsqlconn = new SqlConnection(conn);
       try
       {

              objsqlconn.Open();
              DataSet ds = new DataSet();
              SqlCommand objcmd = new SqlCommand("usp_loadproperties",
objsqlconn);
              objcmd.CommandType = CommandType.StoredProcedure;

              SqlParameter property_id = objcmd.Parameters.Add("@PropertyID",
SqlDbType.Int);
              property_id.Value = 0;

              SqlDataAdapter objAdp = new SqlDataAdapter(objcmd);

              objAdp.Fill(ds);

              grdloadproperties.DataSource = ds;
              grdloadproperties.DataBind();

       }
       catch (Exception ex)
       {
           Response.Write(ex.Message.ToString());
       }
       finally
       {
           objsqlconn.Close();
       }

 }
```

Sample Stored Procedure Insert and Update Query:

```
USE [ado]
GO
/****** Object:  StoredProcedure [dbo].[usp_InsertUpdate]    Script Date:
07/01/2014 00:06:02 ******/
SET ANSI_NULLS ON
GO
SET QUOTED_IDENTIFIER ON
GO
CREATE PROCEDURE [dbo].[usp_InsertUpdate]
    (
    @Employee_ID int,
    @Employee_Name varchar(100),
    @Employee_Address varchar(500),
    @Employee_Sal money
    )
AS
    if(@Employee_ID = 0)
    begin
    Insert into Employee(Employee_Name,Employee_Address,Employee_Salary)

    Values

    (@Employee_Name,@Employee_Address,@Employee_Sal)
    end

    else

    begin

    Update Employee set
Employee_Name=@Employee_Name,Employee_Address=@Employee_Address,Employee_Salary=@Employee_Sal

    Where Employee_ID=@Employee_ID

    end

    RETURN
```

Sample Stored Procedure Delete Query:

```
USE [ado]
GO
/****** Object:  StoredProcedure [dbo].[usp_Delete]    Script Date: 07/01/2014
00:27:35 ******/
SET ANSI_NULLS ON
GO
SET QUOTED_IDENTIFIER ON
GO
CREATE PROCEDURE [dbo].[usp_Delete]
    (
    @Employee_ID int
    )
AS
    Delete from Employee Where Employee_ID = @Employee_ID
    RETURN
```

• • •

5.5 ASP.NET MVC:

Overview of Model-View-Controller

The Model-View-Controller (MVC) is an architectural pattern that separates an application into three main logical components: the model, the view, and the controller. Each of these components are built to handle specific development aspects of an application. MVC is one of the most frequently used industry-standard web development framework to create scalable and extensible projects.

MVC Components

Following are the components of MVC –

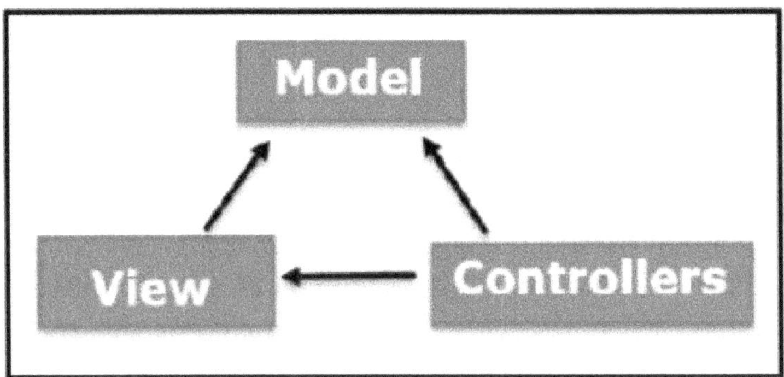

Figure 5.4 : Flow of MVC

Model

- The Model component corresponds to all the data-related logic that the user works with. This can represent either the data that is being transferred between the View and Controller components or any other business logic-related data. For example, a Customer object will retrieve the customer information from the database, manipulate it and update it data back to the database or use it to render data.

View

- The View component is used for all the UI logic of the application. For example, the Customer view will include all the UI components such as text boxes, dropdowns, etc. that the final user interacts with.

Controller

- Controllers act as an interface between Model and View components to process all the business logic and incoming requests, manipulate data using the Model component and interact with the Views to render the final output. For example, the Customer controller will handle all the interactions and inputs from the Customer View and update the database using the Customer Model. The same controller will be used to view the Customer data.

ASP.NET MVC

ASP.NET supports three major development models: Web Pages, Web Forms and MVC (Model View Controller). ASP.NET MVC framework is a lightweight, highly testable presentation framework that is integrated with the existing ASP.NET features, such as master pages, authentication, etc. Within .NET, this framework is defined in the System.Web.Mvc assembly. The latest version of the MVC Framework is 5.0. We use Visual Studio to create ASP.NET MVC applications which can be added as a template in Visual Studio.

ASP.NET MVC Features

ASP.NET MVC provides the following features –

- Ideal for developing complex but lightweight applications.
- Provides an extensible and pluggable framework, which can be easily replaced and customized. For example, if you do not wish to use the in-built Razor or ASPX View Engine, then you can use any other third-party view engines or even customize the existing ones.

- Utilizes the component-based design of the application by logically dividing it into Model, View, and Controller components. This enables the developers to manage the complexity of large-scale projects and work on individual components.
- MVC structure enhances the test-driven development and testability of the application, since all the components can be designed interface-based and tested using mock objects. Hence, ASP.NET MVC Framework is ideal for projects with large team of web developers.
- Supports all the existing vast ASP.NET functionalities, such as Authorization and Authentication, Master Pages, Data Binding, User Controls, Memberships, ASP.NET Routing, etc.
- Does not use the concept of View State (which is present in ASP.NET). This helps in building applications, which are lightweight and gives full control to the developers.

MVC Framework - Architecture

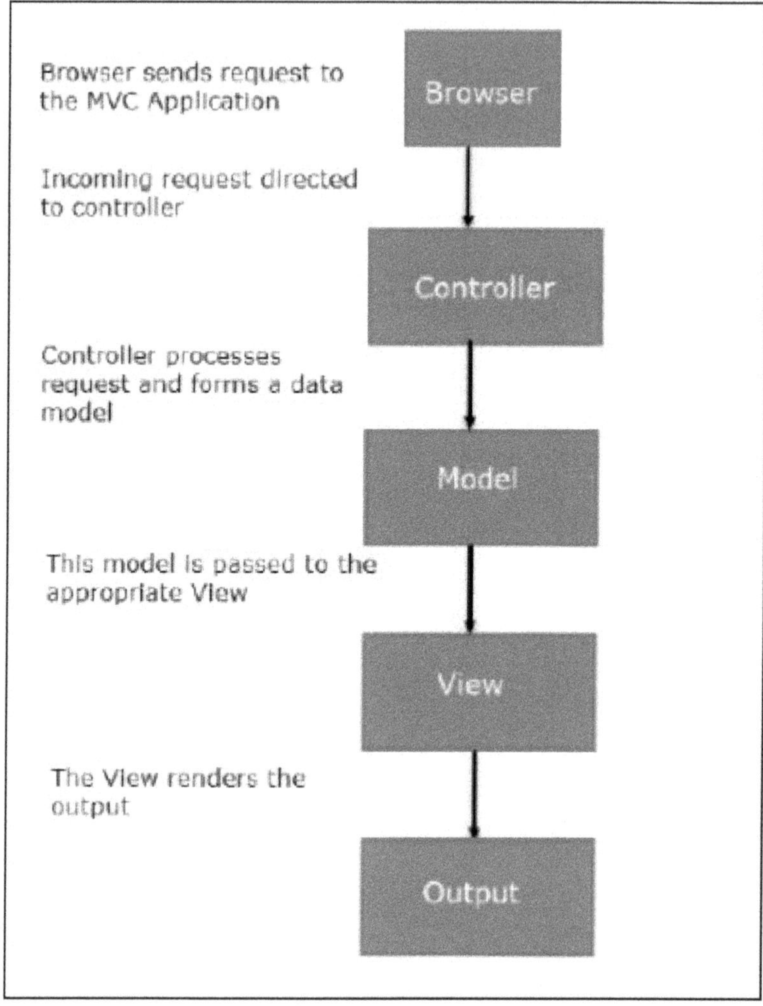

Figure 5-4 : MVC Framework - Architecture

Flow Steps

Step 1 – The client browser sends request to the MVC Application.

Step 2 – Global.ascx receives this request and performs routing based on the URL of the incoming request using the RouteTable, RouteData, UrlRoutingModule and MvcRouteHandler objects.

Step 3 – This routing operation calls the appropriate controller and executes it using the IControllerFactory object and MvcHandler object's Execute method.

Step 4 – The Controller processes the data using Model and invokes the appropriate method using ControllerActionInvoker object

Step 5 – The processed Model is then passed to the View, which in turn renders the final output.

Model in ASP.NET MVC

The model classes represents domain-specific data and business logic in the MVC application. It represents the shape of the data as public properties and business logic as methods.

In the ASP.NET MVC Application, all the Model classes must be created in the Model folder.

Adding a Model Class

Let's create the model class that should have the required properties for the Student entity.

In the MVC application in Visual Studio, and right-click on the Model folder, select Add -> and click on Class... It will open the Add New Item dialog box.

In the Add New Item dialog box, enter the class name Student and click Add.

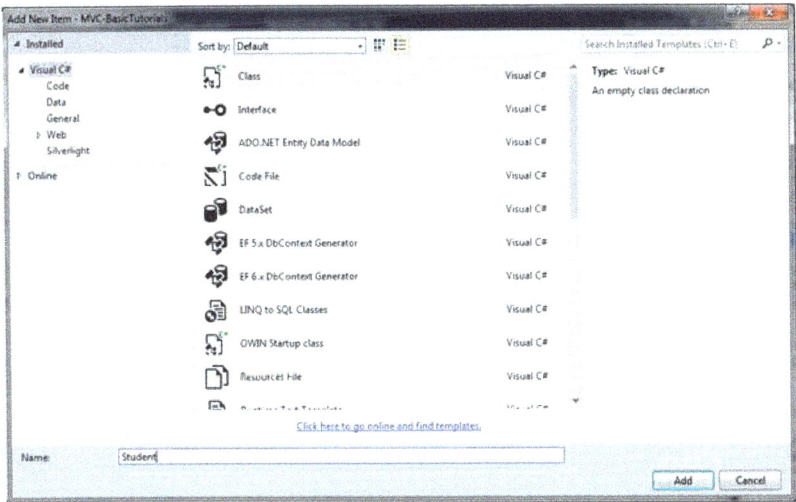

Figure 5-5 : Create Model Class

This will add a new Student class in model folder. We want this model class to store id, name, and age of the students. So, we will have to add public properties for Id, Name, and Age, as shown below.

```
public class Student
{
    public int StudentId { get; set; }
    public string StudentName { get; set;  }
    public int Age { get; set;  }
}
```

The model class can be used in the view to populate the data, as well as sending data to the controller.

View in ASP.NET MVC

In this section, you will learn how to create a view and use the model class in it in the ASP.NET MVC application.

A view is used to display data using the model class object. The Views folder contains all the view files in the ASP.NET MVC application.

A controller can have one or more action methods, and each action method can return a different view. In short, a controller can render one or more views. So, for easy maintenance, the MVC framework requires a separate sub-folder for each controller with the same name as a controller, under the Views folder.

For example, all the views rendered from the HomeController will resides in the Views > Home folder. In the same way, views for StudentController will resides in Views > Student folder, as shown below.

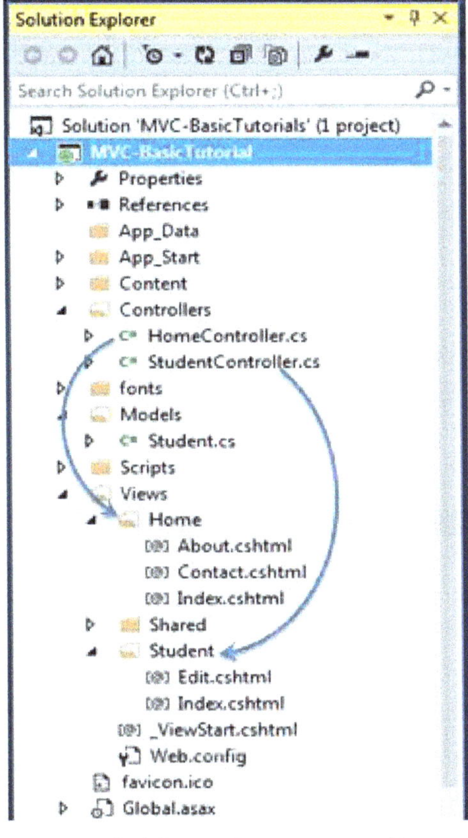

Figure 5-6 : View folders for Controllers

Note:

The Shared folder contains views, layout views, and partial views, which will be shared among multiple controllers.

Controllers in ASP.NET MVC

In this section, you will learn about the Controller in ASP.NET MVC.

The Controller in MVC architecture handles any incoming URL request. The Controller is a class, derived from the base class System.Web.Mvc.Controller. Controller class contains public methods called Action methods. Controller and its action method handles incoming browser requests, retrieves necessary model data and returns appropriate responses.

In ASP.NET MVC, every controller class name must end with a word "Controller". For example, the home page controller name must be HomeController, and for the student page, it must be the StudentController. Also, every controller class must be located in the Controller folder of the MVC folder structure.

Adding a New Controller

In the previous section, we learned how to create our first MVC application, which created a default HomeController. Here, we will create new StudentController class.

In the Visual Studio, right click on the Controller folder -> select Add -> click on Controller..

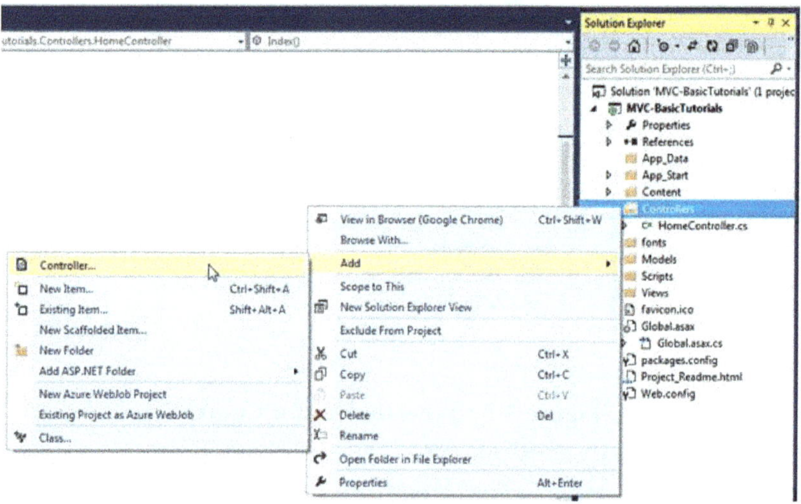

Figure 5-7 : Add New Controller

This opens Add Scaffold dialog, as shown below.

Note:

Scaffolding is an automatic code generation framework for ASP.NET web applications. Scaffolding reduces the time taken to develop a controller, view, etc. in the MVC framework. You can develop a customized scaffolding template using T4 templates as per your architecture and coding standards.

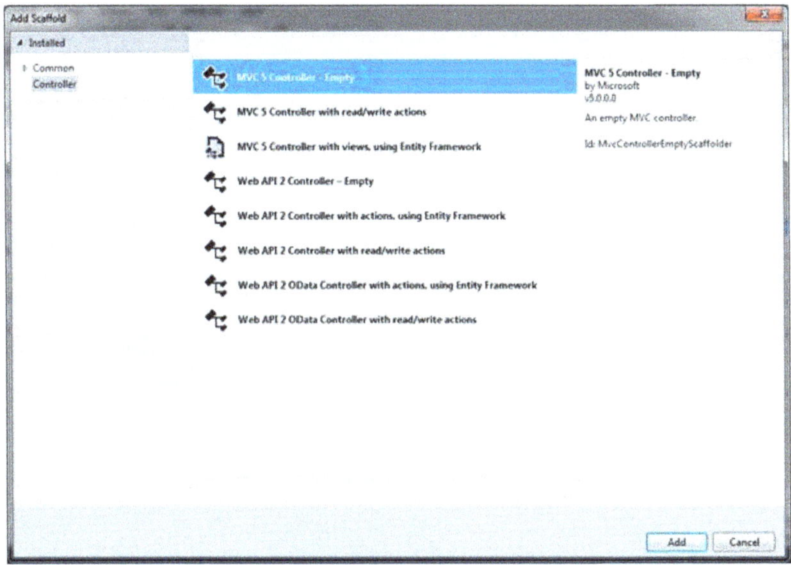

Figure 5-8 : Adding Controller

Add Scaffold dialog contains different templates to create a new controller. We will learn about other templates later. For now, select "MVC 5 Controller - Empty" and click Add. It will open the Add Controller dialog, as shown below

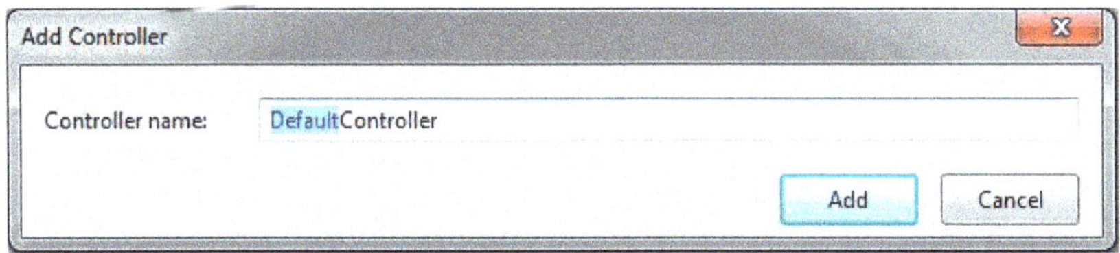

Figure 5-9 : Adding Controller

In the Add Controller dialog, enter the name of the controller. Remember, the controller name must end with Controller. Write StudentController and click Add.

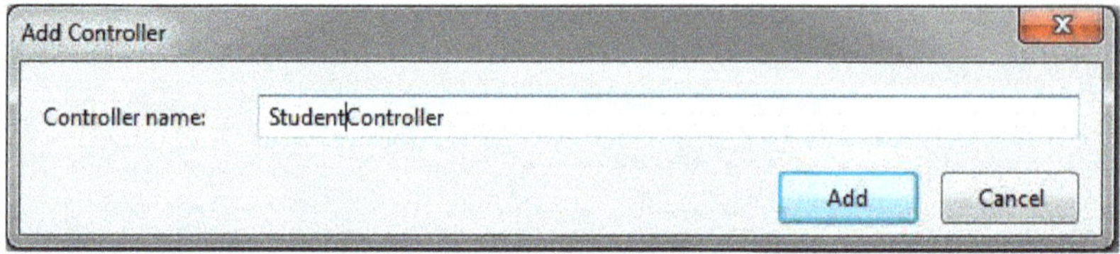

Figure 5-10 : Adding Controller

This will create the StudentController class with the Index() method in StudentController.cs file under the Controllers folder, as shown below.

Example:

Controller

```
using System;
using System.Collections.Generic;
using System.Linq;
using System.Web;
using System.Web.Mvc;

namespace MVC_BasicTutorials.Controllers
{
    public class StudentController : Controller
    {
        // GET: Student
        public ActionResult Index()
        {
            return View();
        }
    }
}
```

As you can see above, the StudentController class is derived from the Controller class. Every controller in MVC must be derived from this abstract Controller class. This base Controller class contains helper methods that can be used for various purposes.

Now, we will return a dummy string from the Index action method of above the StudentController. Changing the return type of Index method from ActionResult to string and returning dummy string is shown below. You will learn about the ActionResult in the next section.

```
using System;
using System.Collections.Generic;
using System.Linq;
using System.Web;
using System.Web.Mvc;

namespace MVC_BasicTutorials.Controllers
{
    public class StudentController : Controller
    {
        // GET: Student
        public string Index()
        {
                return "This is Index action method of StudentController";
        }
    }
}
```

We have already seen in the routing section that the URL request http://localhost/student or http://localhost/student/index is handled by the Index() method of the StudentController class, as shown above. So let's invoke it from the browser and you will see the following page in the browser.

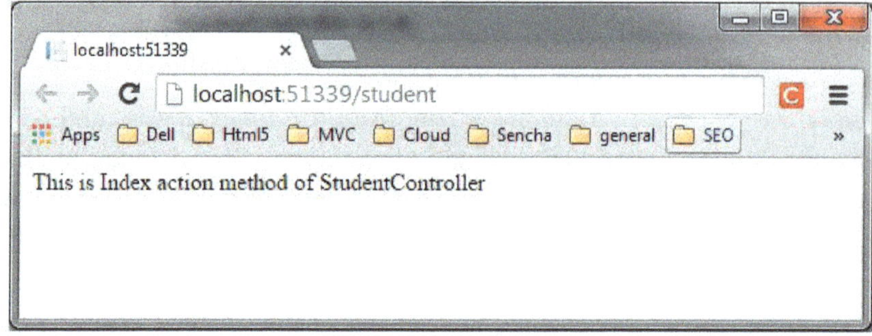

Figure 5-11 : Controller

Points to Remember :

- The Controller handles incoming URL requests. MVC routing sends requests to the appropriate controller and action method based on URL and configured Routes.
- All the public methods in the Controller class are called Action methods.
- The Controller class must be derived from System.Web.Mvc.Controller class.
- The Controller class name must end with "Controller".
- A new controller can be created using different scaffolding templates. You can create a custom scaffolding template also.

• • •

5.6 Routing in MVC

- Routing is not specific to the MVC framework. It can be used with ASP.NET Webform application or MVC application.
- ASP.NET introduced Routing to eliminate the needs of mapping each URL with a physical file. Routing enables us to define a URL pattern that maps to the request handler. This request handler can be a file or class. In ASP.NET Webform application, request handler is .aspx file, and in MVC, it is the Controller class and Action method.

- For example, http://domain/students can be mapped to http://domain/studentsinfo.aspx in ASP.NET Webforms, and the same URL can be mapped to Student Controller and Index action method in MVC.

Route :

Route defines the URL pattern and handler information. All the configured routes of an application stored in RouteTable and will be used by the Routing engine to determine appropriate handler class or file for an incoming request.

The following figure illustrates the Routing process.

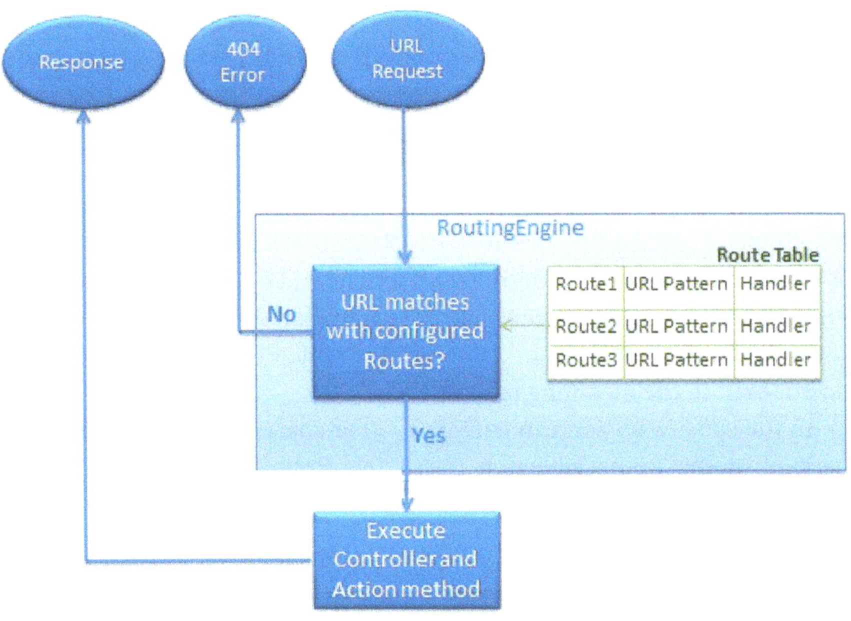

Figure 5-12 : Routing in MVC

Configure a Route

Every MVC application must configure (register) at least one route configured by the MVC framework by default. You can register a route in

RouteConfig class, which is in RouteConfig.cs under App_Start folder. The following figure illustrates how to configure a route in the RouteConfig class .

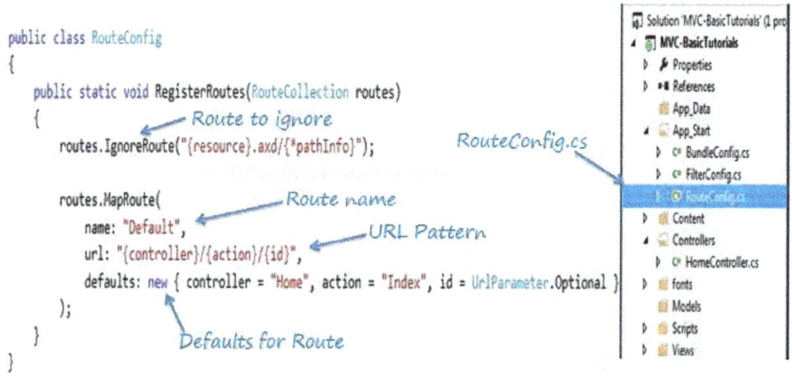

```
public class RouteConfig
{
    public static void RegisterRoutes(RouteCollection routes)
    {
        routes.IgnoreRoute("{resource}.axd/{*pathInfo}");

        routes.MapRoute(
            name: "Default",
            url: "{controller}/{action}/{id}",
            defaults: new { controller = "Home", action = "Index", id = UrlParameter.Optional }
        );
    }
}
```

Figure 5-13 : Configure Routes in MVC

As you can see in the above figure, the route is configured using the MapRoute() extension method of RouteCollection, where name is "Default", url pattern is "{controller}/{action}/{id}" and defaults parameter for controller, action method and id parameter. Defaults specify which controller, action method, or value of id parameter should be used if they do not exist in the incoming request URL.

In the same way, you can configure other routes using the MapRoute() method of the RouteCollection class. This RouteCollection is actually a property of the RouteTable class

URL Pattern

The URL pattern is considered only after the domain name part in the URL. For example, the URL pattern "{controller}/{action}/{id}" would look like localhost:1234/{controller}/{action}/{id}. Anything after "localhost:1234/" would be considered as a controller name. The same way, anything after the controller name would be considered as action name and then the value of id parameter.

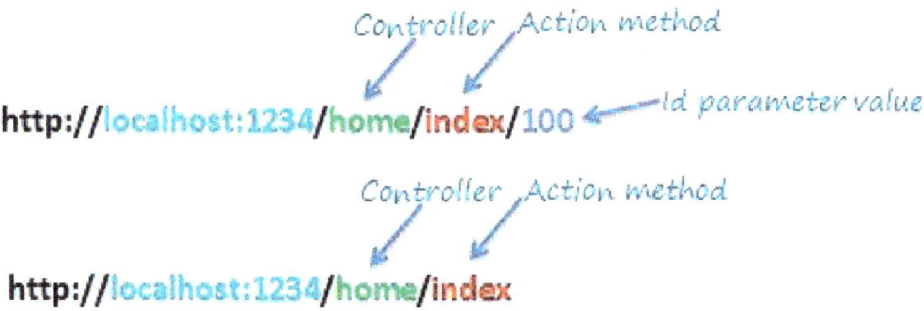

Figure 5-14 : Routing in MVC

If the URL doesn't contain anything after the domain name, then the default controller and action method will handle the request. For example, http://localhost:1234 would be handled by the HomeController and the Index() method as configured in the default parameter.

The following table shows which Controller, Action method, and Id parameter would handle different URLs considering the above default route.

URL	Controller	Action	Id
http://localhost/home	HomeController	Index	null
http://localhost/home/index/123	HomeController	Index	123
http://localhost/home/about	HomeController	About	null
http://localhost/home/contact	HomeController	Contact	null
http://localhost/student	StudentController	Index	null
http://localhost/student/edit/123	StudentController	Edit	123

Table 5-2 : URL Pattern

CHAPTER VI

Practical List

1. Create a web application to display "Welcome to the world of ASP.NET" on web browser when user "Click" button is clicked.
2. Create a web page in which user can enter enrollment no, student name and marks of 5 subjects. Calculate total, percentage and grade of student and display it. [Use text box, label, button control].
3. Write a program to enable - disable textbox and change width of text box programmatically in ASP.Net.
4. Create a web page that will take two radio buttons labeled as a gender, if user selects radio button the gender will be changed according to selected radio button.
5. Write a program which have list box and image controls, list box is used to display items and when user clicks on item in list box it display the item image in image control.
6. Create a web page for registration which have name, dob, gender, email id, contact no, address, city, pin code, hobbies and display all data in same page with proper layout.
7. Write a program that uses a textbox for a user input and validate it using required field validation.
8. Create a web page for registration which have name, dob, gender, email id, contact no, address, city, pin code, hobbies. After the user enters the appropriate values the validate button must validates the values entered and display all data in same page with proper layout.
9. Write a program to check the length of the string in the text box using custom validation.
10. Create a master page that contain links for home page, about us page and contact page, when user clicks on particular link it will display that particular page.
11. Create a web application for registration system that contains navigation control to specify link like registration and login. When user click registration link user should be navigated to registration page. When user click on the login link login page will be display that will redirected to registration page if user logged in to system. [Use master page and

session to maintain the user identity].

12. Write a program that has a form taking the user's name as input. Store this name in a permanent cookie & whenever the page is opened again, then value of the name field should be attached with the cookie's content.
13. Create student database which contain table stud_registration and have fields like first name, last name, dob, email id, contact number, gender, address, city, pin code.
14. Create web application which will insert, view, search, update, and delete records from stud_registration table. [Use gridview] . stud_registration sample data

First Name	Last Name	DOB	Email	Contact Number	Gender	Address	City	Pin code
Paul	Walker	1/1/90	walker@gmail.com	9876543210	M	Nadiad	Nadiad	387001
Sam	Watson	2/2/85	sam.w@yahoo.com	9876543210	M	Surat	Surat	390014

stud_registration sample data

15. Create a web application with validation which will insert, view, search, update and delete records from table. [Use listview] product_info sample data

ID	Name	Quantity	Price
1	TV	200	21000
2	AC	100	16000

product_info sample data

16. Create table employee with the following columns and data types.

Columns	Data Type
dept_id	Int
Name	nvarchar(20)
Doj	Datetime
Salary	Float
Designation	nvarchar(30)

- Insert following records into the table

dept_id	name	Doj	Salary	Designation
D1	Kaushal	1/1/2014	10000	Developer
D2	Ansh	2/2/2013	12000	Tester
D3	Eahul	3/3/2012	15000	Analyst

- Change the candidate name from "Ansh" to "Alpesh".
- Select records from table where salary > 10000 and display it.

17. Create database train_master having table train_info and have fields like train_id (PK, AI), train_name, train_type, arrival_time, departure_time, start_location, end _location.
18. Create database train_master having table train_info and have fields like train_id (PK, AI), train_name, train_type, arrival_time, departure_time, start_location, end _location.
19. Create a Calendar Navigation by using Ajax Calendar Extender control ,in which user can Navigate Year , Month and select date from the Calendar control.
20. Create an application which reads data from an XML file and also write data to the file.
21. Create database book_master having table book_info and have fields like book_id (PK, AI), book_name, author, price. Create a web application with validation which will insert, view, search, update and delete records from table. [Use MVC architecture]
22. Create a data driven website system from following list.

    - College Web Portal
    - E shopping
    - Online Student Management
    - Online Inventory
    - Web Time Sheet
    - Complain Management
    - Alumni Information System

- Property Management
- Online Hotel Booking
- Library Management
- Hospital Management

CHAPTER VII

Question Bank

Chapter 1 : Introduction

1. Explain .NET Framework with proper diagram.
2. What is MSIL?Explain with Daigram.
3. Write a short note on .NET framework class library.
4. Explain CLR, CLS, CTS.
5. What is JIT compiler?

• • •

Chapter 2 : ASP.NET Controls, UI Design & Coding

1. Explain Server Control properties in detail.
2. Explain HTML server controls in brief.
3. List out different web controls and explain any 5 with example.
4. What is web page? Explain with example.
5. Create a web application that performs the basic operations of calculator.

• • •

Chapter 3 : ASP.NET Validation Controls, State Management & Navigation

1. List out different validation controls. Explain each in brief.
2. What is state management? Why state management is required?
3. Write a short note on session state.
4. Explain client based state.
5. What is master page and content page? What is the use of master page? Explain with example.

• • •

Chapter 4 : Data Access through ADO.NET

1. What is ADO.net? Explain ADO.net architecture.
2. What is connection string? What is the use of connection string?
3. Explain various DataSource Controls.
4. Write a short note on DbCommand.
5. Explain gridview and list view controls in detail.

• • •

Chapter 5 : Advanced ASP.NET

1. What is MVC? Explain MVC architecture.
2. Explain LINQ in detail.
3. What is stored procedure? Write down advantages of it.
4. Write a stored procedure for insert.
5. Explain LINQ to XML.

www.ingramcontent.com/pod-product-compliance
Ingram Content Group UK Ltd.
Pitfield, Milton Keynes, MK11 3LW, UK
UKHW021830270726
14058UKWH00001B/76

9 798886 062106